"*Uncommon Answers* reve[al]
door to miracles, proving t[hat]
With compelling stories and biblical wisdom, Shrodes challenges the
notion that miracles are rare."

Mark Batterson, *New York Times* bestselling
author of *The Circle Maker*

"*Uncommon Answers* is an exciting journey of understanding what
it's like to partner with God in prayer and obedience . . . and then
watch Him do the impossible! I pray that the miracles you read about
in this book will elevate your faith to believe God to do exceedingly
abundantly above all that you could ever ask or imagine in your life!"

Doug Clay, general superintendent, General
Council of the Assemblies of God

"A faith-building book about the miracles God performs in answer to
prayer, as well as a strategic manual about how to surrender your whole
life to God. You will certainly be blessed and challenged!"

Donna L. Barrett, general secretary, General Council
of the Assemblies of God

"Dr. Shrodes's honesty and vulnerability demonstrate that miracles
and extraordinary answers to prayer are still relevant today. Weaving
together personal stories, accounts from others, and scriptural narratives, she guides readers toward deeper surrender and collaboration
with the Holy Spirit, fostering spiritual growth and transformation."

Dr. Chris Corbett, chair and professor of religion, Barnett College of
Ministry and Theology, Southeastern University

"I remember when Dr. Shrodes shared her tenacious journey of finding
her biological father. I watched as God reunited them in an extraordinary way. If you question whether God hears you, let this book be your
proof. God does hear us—He just responds with uncommon answers."

Dr. Saehee Duran, ordained minister with
the Assemblies of God U.S.A.

"No matter how big the challenge you are facing, God has an uncommon answer for your prayers. Dr. Deanna Shrodes will equip you to
supercharge your prayers and inspire you with many miracle stories
from her own life, from Scripture, and from others who have experienced God's uncommon answers."

Alan J. Ehler, pastor; professor; author,
How to Make Big Decisions Wisely

"Many good books change our thinking. More importantly, a few change our doing. I have been partnering with the Holy Spirit most of my adult life. Dr. Deanna Shrodes has given me opportunity to change the way I do my partnering. For a lifelong classical Pentecostal, that is rare and helpful indeed. Usually, answers are more important than questions. Shrodes's answers are uncommon."

Dr. Terry Raburn, superintendent, Peninsular Florida
District Council of the Assemblies of God

"Dr. Deanna Doss Shrodes mines rich biblical truths and offers colorful (and sometimes gritty) life-in-the-real-world stories that poignantly point the way to finding our own uncommon answers to the prayers we've prayed in darkness and desperation. Your heart will become primed to receive the 'extraordinarily more' God has in store."

Dr. Jodi Detrick, former columnist, *The Seattle Times*; author, *The Jesus-Hearted Woman* and *The Settled Soul*

"Dr. Shrodes normalizes the uncommon reality of living 'by His Spirit.' She weaves real-life examples, biblical narratives, and practical applications, giving wings to the miraculous in daily living. You will find yourself shouting as you read, 'This is for me!' These pages unveil the true hope for our world."

Crystal M. Martin, missionary, Assemblies of God World Missions;
speaker; author, *Women in Ministry Mission Critical*

"Readers will witness a remarkable journey of faith, hope, and divine intervention. Deanna masterfully intertwines the extraordinary story of finding her birth father with the truth of Scripture and practical tools for the reader to experience uncommon answers in their own life."

Nonda Houston, national director, AG Women

"Deanna beautifully pairs God's uncommon provision with very personal desperations. It's a joy to read this writer's heart. What a journey of unconventional faith as she underlines how Jesus can meet our needs, enabling us to see His presence daily in a not-so-common way."

Sue Duffield, singer; author; host, *Suebiquitous Podcast*

"Are you asking God for a miracle? *Uncommon Answers* reminds us that the miraculous is commonplace to God. Dr. Deanna shares her personal story and practical truths that guide us out of ordinary, mundane faith and into audacious faith that believes God for anything."

Angela Donadio, founder, Communicators' Collective; author,
Brave Enough to Believe, *Fearless*, and more

UNCOMMON
Answers

UN COM MON
Answers

Partnering
with the
Holy Spirit
to **Receive
Extraordinarily
More**

DEANNA DOSS SHRODES

Chosen

a division of Baker Publishing Group
Minneapolis, Minnesota

Library of Congress Cataloging-in-Publication Data
Names: Shrodes, Deanna Doss, 1966– author.
Title: Uncommon answers : partnering with the Holy Spirit to receive extraordinarily more / Deanna Doss Shrodes.
Description: Minneapolis, Minnesota : Chosen Books, a division of Baker Publishing Group, [2025] | Includes bibliographical references.
Identifiers: LCCN 2024026739 | ISBN 9780800772994 (paper) | ISBN 9780800773069 (casebound) | ISBN 9781493448845 (ebook)
Subjects: LCSH: Christian women—Conduct of life. | Women—Religious life.
Classification: LCC BV4527 .S438 2025 | DDC 248.8/43—dc23/eng/20240807
LC record available at https://lccn.loc.gov/2024026739

25 26 27 28 29 30 31   7 6 5 4 3 2 1

For Livvy
God loves you.
He has a plan for your life.
His hand is on your life.
I love you,
Dee Dee

CONTENTS

FOREWORD

For several years I prayed for a specific financial need related to my overseas ministry. Missionary work has always been a challenge for me because I'm certainly not a professional fundraiser, and most people don't spend a lot of time thinking about needs in developing countries.

Eventually I hit a spiritual wall. I was discouraged. I had prayed and prayed and prayed again. Yet it seemed like the promised provision was just trickling in. I needed a miracle, but I felt too exhausted to keep fighting.

A friend of mine who is an intercessor kept encouraging me with words of hope. I decided to fast and pray for a few days, and then my wife and a few other intercessors joined in for a time of fasting and focused prayer. I also texted other friends who agreed to pray with me for a breakthrough. Much like Aaron and Hur, who held up Moses's arms during battle, my friends stood with me.

I often parked in Matthew 7:7 and meditated on those words. This verse says, "Ask, and it will be given to you; seek, and you will find; knock, and it will be opened to you" (NASB). Jesus gave us this ironclad promise. But He didn't spell out a time frame for when prayers are answered. He didn't say, "Ask, and it will be given to you in two weeks," or "Seek, and you will find in twenty-four hours." We must leave the timing of the answer in God's hands.

Thankfully, after my friends prayed with us about the financial need, a dam broke. Money began to flow. Over a period of weeks, enough funds came in to complete several of our overseas projects. Half the budget was met in a matter of days. And my faith grew stronger in the process.

I experienced an uncommon answer!

That's what this book is about. Deanna Doss Shrodes masterfully shares from her own life, and from Scripture, about how God releases His miracles in response to our requests. If you are standing in faith for an answer from God, this book is for you—especially if you have been waiting a long time for that miracle.

Waiting is painful. We want our answer now! But we forget that patience is part of the process of receiving answers from God. Never forget that many people in the Bible waited a long time for the fulfillment of God's promises:

- Sarah waited twenty-five years from the time God told Abraham that he and his wife would have a son until the day Isaac was born.
- Moses waited forty years in the wilderness before God called him to deliver Israel from the Egyptians.
- Caleb waited forty-five years from the time God promised him that Israel would take Canaan until the moment he received Hebron as his inheritance.

- Hannah endured unspecified years of barrenness waiting for her baby, Samuel.
- David waited at least fifteen years from the time he was anointed to be a leader until he became king. It was David who wrote these words during his long delay: "I waited patiently and expectantly for the LORD; and He inclined to me and heard my cry" (Psalm 40:1 AMP).

God gives us a promise—that's the easy part. But faith also involves warfare. The devil hurls doubts and obstacles in our direction. And there are always, always delays. It is in those painful times of waiting when we are most tempted to quit.

Are you waiting for a prayer to be answered? Have you considered throwing in the towel? I believe that by the time you finish this book, your faith will be bigger and you will have more patience for your prayer journey.

Zerubbabel and Joshua, the two men commissioned to rebuild Solomon's temple, struggled with intense discouragement as they looked at Jerusalem's ruins. The task was overwhelming, the cost was prohibitive, the workers were dismayed, and their enemies were fierce.

They started the work in earnest, but they heard a familiar voice that whispered, "You'll never finish this. God is going to abandon you in the middle of this project." Fortunately, the prophet Haggai showed up with a refreshing announcement. He told them: "'But now take courage . . . and work; for I am with you,' declares the LORD" (Haggai 2:4 NASB).

The Lord promised He would see the building project to completion. He said: "The latter glory of this house will be greater than the former . . . and in this place I will give peace" (v. 9 NASB). Those prophetic promises propelled Zerubbabel and Joshua forward. Their passion was refueled. Their hands grew strong again, and they returned to the work. God's glorious house arose from an ash heap.

Uncommon Answers brings the same kind of encouragement that Haggai provided. Like Haggai, this book offers a word of hope: "Take courage! The Lord is with you!" Don't rush through this book. Meditate on the promises included in each chapter and let the Holy Spirit speak to you. Uncommon answers are on the way!

J. Lee Grady, author, traveling minister, and
director of The Mordecai Project

INTRODUCTION

My guess is that you've picked up this book because you need an answer to prayer or a miracle of some kind. You're in good company. I'm hard-pressed to think of even one person I know who isn't waiting for something from God. For many of those people, the answer they need requires a miracle. A great need is required for a miracle. So if you're in that place today where you're desperate for a miracle, know that God is still doing them today—you're going to receive plenty of proof of that in this book.

Prayer is the most effective strategy for receiving an answer from God. Are there other biblical strategies that can be combined with prayer to, in effect, "supercharge" your prayers? In my and many other believers' firsthand experience, yes. In this book I'm going to take you on a journey of understanding what it is like to take additional tangible steps in obedience to God's direction to see extraordinarily more happen in your life and in the lives of those you are praying for. I'll share verified miracle stories in which partnering with the Holy Spirit was part of receiving an extraordinary answer.

Sharing the stories in this book is not an attempt to glorify individuals. If you read them and think, *Wow, what special people, it was so great of God to do that for them,* you've missed the point. Every chapter you're about to read was written with the purpose of showing what is possible for you and *your* situation.

As you read about the verified miracles and answers to prayer, you may be tempted to think, *But these are just outliers. What happened to them isn't what usually happens.* What if what usually happens was never meant to be what usually happens? Perhaps we have it all backward.

I was reading a medical book when a sentence seemed to leap off the page. The author referenced circumstances where people overcame grim medical prognoses, ones that were normally fatal. Of those outliers, the ones who received a miracle, she wrote, "It stands to reason that if there is one exception to a theory, perhaps the theory is not entirely correct, no matter how long it has been accepted as truth."[1] She then went on a quest to find out what those who were the exception to the rule did differently. *Uncommon Answers* does the same thing, but from a spiritual sense, not a medical one. How do some believers walk in extraordinarily more?

In the coming pages, we will look at what some may be tempted to call outliers, to discover ways they partnered with the Holy Spirit before their miracle, in order to learn from them. I believe God has extraordinarily more for you as you partner with the Holy Spirit. May God bless you on this exciting journey.

1

UNCOMMON ANSWERS DON'T HAVE TO BE RARE

To get us started on this exploration of uncommon answers, I'm going to tell you about the greatest uncommon answer to prayer I ever received. It was such an uncommon answer—an extraordinary, verified miracle—that it was reported by CBS News and many other national and international news media outlets. To get there, we need to wind the clock back to 1965.

My mother was a single American woman from Richmond, Virginia, who became pregnant and experienced intense rejection by her family. Her parents did not approve of her relationship with my father, and she was kicked out of the family home. With nowhere else to turn, she ended up at a maternity home a few hours away. In August of 1966, she gave birth to me and named me Melanie Lynn. We were separately transported back to Richmond, Virginia, where I would become a foster child. She took forty-seven days to make up her mind and sign the relinquishment papers. She placed me for adoption realizing that she had no way to care for me. Her parents made it clear: She was not welcome to return to the family if I was with her. She would try to rebuild her life, with no one aware of her pregnancy or my existence.

After several months a Christian couple, also in Virginia, adopted me. My adoptive parents legally changed my name to Deanna. They didn't know anyone by that name, nor was there any particular reason they gave me this name; they simply liked the name and felt drawn to it. I was raised in a Pentecostal home, accepted Jesus at an early age, and sensed a call to the ministry.

I wondered about my birth parents all my life. When I became pregnant with our first son, I had an insatiable yearning to know my roots. After several years of searching and some miracles thrown in along the way, I reunited with my birth mother when I was twenty-seven years old. Upon our reunion, I learned that my birth father was 100 percent Greek and much older than my mother, one of the reasons her parents did not approve. She was still angry, twenty-seven years later, that he had not supported her during that time. I could understand that. She didn't want to speak of him, other than telling me he was Greek and I looked just like him. That was all the further she would go.

The two of us had a wonderful relationship for several decades, as long as I didn't bring up the subject of my father. I was the mother of her only grandchildren, with whom she also had a good relationship. She didn't want anything to mess that up. She often quipped, "Life is good!" and she wanted to keep it that way.

The longing to know who my father was, and to know him personally, never left me. Realizing he was at least a decade older than my mother, I decided in 2013 that it was time to raise the question again. If he was not already deceased, he likely soon would be. I carefully broached the subject, and she responded that she was never going to tell me who he was. I reminded her that he would be at least in his eighties by this point, and asked if she would reconsider, knowing how much this meant to me and that (by her own admission) I had been so good to her for the last twenty years.

"What don't you understand?" she railed. "I'm never going to tell you who he is! I will go to the grave with his name." Just a few weeks later, she was diagnosed with bile duct cancer. None of us—including her—knew she was sick. It quickly took her life, and true to her word, she took my father's name to the grave.

I had already DNA tested with all of the major companies at the time. My mother was telling the truth, my father was 100 percent Greek—my DNA report informed me that I was half Greek. I had hundreds of matches on my maternal side, mostly descendants of people from Virginia. But I had no close matches on my paternal side, and the three or four Greek matches I did have were so distant that it was impossible to identify any close relatives. Without a miracle, even if I discovered my father's identity, I would find a grave and not a man. Undaunted, I continually prayed and searched.

There were days I was despondent, feeling as if time was running out to find my father alive. So I did something I had never done before—I took a forty-day leave of absence from work to go away by myself to grieve, rest, and recover. I was devastated that my birth mother had died. I was also grieving the information she took with her.

Every day for forty days I ate, slept, prayed, read God's Word, journaled, walked a few miles, and went to church on Sundays. During this time, I prayed something I had asked of God many times over the years—that if I was not able to find my father in time, He would send someone who would lead him to Jesus, in the hope that not only would he have eternal life but that I might someday meet him in heaven.

One day as I continued in prayer, I had this simple thought: *I really believe what I believe.* I am not just a Pentecostal in name, but in practice. I have been given one or more of His gifts (1 Corinthians 12:8–10), and I had witnessed hundreds, possibly thousands, of individuals exhibit His gifts also. I had both experienced and witnessed signs and wonders as Scripture speaks of, up close and personal. Suddenly I had an idea for a new prayer.

> *Lord, You know I believe. This is not just what my church believed when I was growing up—this is my faith. I believe what I preach. And so, God, as I lie here on this floor crying out to You, I ask You for one thing: Give me a name! Give me my father's name.*

For three days this was my cry to God as I repeated this request: Give me the name. And on the third day, He did. The

Holy Spirit dropped a thought into my mind: *Your father's name is Gus.*

I did not broadcast this to the masses (yet), but I did share it with people who were close to me, namely my husband, my best friend, and a few others. By this time, I had assembled a team of friends and acquaintances as a search team to identify my father. We called ourselves "Finding Mr. Greek," and had a private group by that name on Facebook. We shared information, tips, and techniques that we would utilize to search. There were a number of unbelievers on the search team as well as believers. A few were atheists. I didn't necessarily seek out people who were Christians, but people who had expertise in DNA, genealogy, searching, and the like.

I let those assisting in the search at the time know that I heard God tell me that my father's name was Gus. I knew that some might think I was flat-out crazy and wasting their time to try to search for a man named Gus because "God said so." Nevertheless, no one laughed. No one scoffed. No one said, "Forget it, I'm not doing this. It's ludicrous." An atheist friend who was serving on the team said, "You're right, I don't believe in God. But you know what? I believe in you—so let's do this!" And we started running after a Greek man named Gus with all our might.

For a year we chased after every man named Gus who lived in Richmond, Virginia, in 1965, within a ten-year age range of my mother in either direction—ten years younger or older. Once we identified men who fit the description, I would call them personally, or call one of their family members, share my story, and ask if they would take a DNA test at my expense. Amazingly, most of them did it. At the end of the year, we had exhausted every possibility for a Gus within a ten-year age range of my mother. It was time for me to admit to the team that I may not have heard from God. I apologized and asked them to forgive me for wasting their time. They were gracious.

For the next nine years, we chased leads for other Greek men who were living in the Richmond area at the time of my conception. I never gave up fervently praying, and a group of friends didn't either. At least one person on the team was working on the search every day, from all over the world. Most of our team members were in America, but we had one as far away as Paraguay. We had thousands of leads, and many more DNA tests that were taken, but no one was a match—until May 11, 2022.

I was on a leadership Zoom call that day that lasted three hours. I had invited Pastor Stephanie Smith of Seattle, Washington, to be our guest instructor on the call. At the close of our time together she said, "I want each of you to take out a piece of paper and write a question to the Lord. This is just between you and God, you will not be sharing it with the group." I took out my paper and wrote, "When are you going to help me find my father?" Unbeknownst to me, my friend Pastor Kristi Hahn had written as one of her questions, "Will you help Deanna find her father?"

When the Zoom call concluded, Regina Zimberlin, one of the lead searchers on our team, called. "Deanna! I have been waiting to tell you that you have a Greek DNA match, and it is a close one! This is it! We're likely going to know who your father is within an hour! We are building your match's family tree right now." As the family tree was quickly assembled, we realized there was only one son in this particular family. That meant identifying my father was quite easy. Can you guess what the son's name was? Gus. Our team was doing a virtual happy dance all over the world.

Two things can be gleaned from what took place that day.

First, don't ever stop praying! People have asked me, "Hadn't you already prayed and asked the Lord countless times?" Yes! Don't ever give up. Second, who you surround yourself with is particularly important. Do you have friends who will stand with you in prayer and not dismiss what is paramount to you? There were a few people in my life who thought the search for my father was unnecessary, or even wrong. Kristi wasn't one of them. She stood with me in prayer for many years.

How did we miss Gus in our search? We didn't go far enough. My mother was twenty at the time of my birth, Gus was thirty-six. If we had extended the search six years further, we would have found him.

Then, imagine my shock to find that Gus was still alive. He was ninety-one years old and in a nursing home, still residing in Richmond. Even more astounding, we found that he had never married, and never had other children—I was his only child!

In less than twenty-four hours, we were on FaceTime together. It was an emotional first call. He immediately accepted me as his daughter (although we would—at my insistence and his full agreement—take a legal paternity test to confirm). Seeing that his eyes were filling with tears, I said, "Gus, I've known for a long time that I was coming for you, but you had no idea. I can see this is a little overwhelming for you. Would you like me to give you some time and call back?"

His next words were, "How soon can you come?"

My husband and I quickly arranged to make the trip from Tampa to be at his side in the nursing home. We discovered that several months previous he had taken a fall at his home. With no one to check on him, he was not readily discovered. But his insightful and kind primary care doctor had a hunch something might be wrong when he didn't show up to an appointment, and a wellness check was made to his home. The police found him on the floor. He recovered for two months in the hospital and then went to the nursing home. Because he could no longer care for himself, he became a ward of Adult Protective Services. They deemed that for his safety, he would remain at the nursing home, where he would receive the full-time care he needed.

The first day I met Gus, I talked to him about where he would spend eternity. I said, "Gus, I'm meeting you at the last part of your life. I have no idea how much time we will have together, I hope it's a lot. The good news is that you and I can spend eternity together, but that's your choice." I explained that accepting Jesus and a relationship with Him would mean eternal life and seeing one another for all eternity. He haltingly said, "I want to make that choice." He prayed the prayer of salvation with me as tears streamed down his face.

Larry and I began making regular trips to Richmond to be at Gus's bedside. I would show up right as the sun was rising and stay most days until it was time for him to go to bed. I was grateful for the flexibility of my work as a statewide women's ministry director. I could work from the road, or at Gus's bedside. From the second we met, we cherished each moment, not knowing how much time we would be granted.

After several weeks it became apparent that in order to have all the time we needed together, Gus would have to come with me back home to Tampa. I jumped through all the hoops necessary with Adult Protective Services and his doctor to be able to bring him home. He required full-time care; we brought in extra caregivers.

During the time we had together, my ninety-one-year-old father grew immensely in God. I learned that no matter how old a person is, change through Christ is possible. I watched Gus go from a tough man to a tender one, who would ask me to read him chapters of the Bible or listen to worship music for hours on end. We took Communion together. In the remaining months of life, he learned everything from the power of prayer to the fruit of the Spirit to the gifts of the Spirit to the Beatitudes, and so much more. In short, I had the privilege of discipling my ninety-one-year-old father.

He died in my arms on December 6, 2022.

Finding Gus, leading him to salvation, discipling him, and tenderly caring for him until he took his last breath was the greatest miracle and privilege of my life. Our story has gone around the world not only to inspire many people but to lead them to Christ.

What's in a Name?

God is totally in the details. Remember that my birth mother named me Melanie Lynn? Melanie is a Greek name that means black or dark. I began my life's journey in darkness—a bleak situation. My parents adopted me and changed my name to Deanna Lynn. They didn't realize how significant their choice was. The name Deanna means divine, valley, or church leader. I became a church leader in my late teen years and have been so for the vast majority of my life, the last eleven years in a full-time denominational role. I often say, "The enemy has a plot, but God has a plan!" I believe my very name was a prophetic foreshadow of that plan.

To receive the most extraordinary answer to prayer I have ever received required not only prayer but a host of other things—listening, waiting, obeying, sacrificing, surrendering, tenacity, and much more. In this book we will explore all of these biblical strategies and more to help you supercharge your prayers. Buckle up and hold on, friend, because you're about to move into the realm of "extraordinarily more"!

The Bible and Uncommon Answers

Scriptural insight regarding uncommon answers will be woven throughout every chapter in this book. However, I'm going to share a few key biblical truths now to lay a foundation as we begin our journey together.

Miraculous answers to prayer occurred throughout the Bible. John 21:25 (KJV) says, "And there are also many other things which Jesus did, the which, if they should be written every one, I suppose that even the world itself could not contain the books that should be written." Jesus did so many things during His time on earth that John said all the world's books did not have the capacity to hold the details!

Jesus wasn't a Lone Ranger type of leader. He was an expert team builder. He always took people with Him, aside from His times of solitude when He went alone to pray and rest. He not only taught His disciples about believing big and seeing extraordinary answers to prayer as normative, but empowered and released them to follow in His footsteps. The book of Acts reports that the apostles regularly saw miracles and extraordinary answers to prayer in their everyday lives (Acts 5:12). Philip, Paul, Stephen, and many others experienced miracles with regularity.

God never intended an uncommon answer to prayer to be for a chosen few. As mentioned, the purpose of this book is not to highlight wonderful things that have happened for a few people. It's to fire you up to believe that extraordinarily more is yours through partnering with the Holy Spirit.

In Acts 10:34, Peter explained to the Gentiles that God is no respecter of persons. The word *respecter* here means "the act of showing favor to one on account of rank, family, wealth, or partiality arising from any cause."[1] This means that no matter what family you come from, how much money you have, or any other reason or partiality you could think of ("arising from any cause"), God shows no favoritism. What He does for one person, He longs to do for all. Miracles should not pertain only to the outliers.

Uncommon answers aren't uncommon because God wants them to be. They are uncommon because people have decided they will be. One reason uncommon answers are rare is because of a lack of asking. How many things have we failed to ask God to do because we assume it's too hard or impossible? God wants us to pray audacious prayers that sound outlandish to many people. We need to pray boldly, reminding ourselves that nothing and no one is bigger than God. As author Mark Batterson says, "Bold prayers honor God, and God honors bold prayers. God isn't offended by your biggest dreams or boldest prayers. He is offended by anything less."[2]

The book of James gives *lack of asking* as a reason for unanswered prayer (James 4:2). It also tells us that sometimes we don't receive because we ask with wrong motives (James 4:2–3). Having a rightly motivated prayer is imperative. Before you pray, ask yourself this question: If this prayer is answered, is it for the glory of God and the good of other people? We know in our heart of hearts that our desire should be to bring glory to His name and be of help to other people. If it isn't, we are asking for selfish gain.

Salvation and Uncommon Answers

Praying to Jesus and receiving forgiveness of sins and eternal life is different from a prayer unrelated to salvation, such as asking for help to make next month's mortgage payment.

Salvation is based on what Jesus has done for us. We can't earn our salvation; it is received by grace through faith. As the apostle Paul explained:

> God saved you by his grace when you believed. And you can't take credit for this; it is a gift from God. Salvation is not a reward for the good things we have done, so none of us can boast about it.
>
> Ephesians 2:8–9

28

As we come to a place where we believe that Jesus is the Son of God, confess our sin to Him, and accept Him as Savior and Lord, we receive the miraculous gift of eternal life. It is a free gift, to us, but it wasn't free for Jesus; it cost Him everything.

The point here is that prayer for salvation and prayer for breakthrough are two different things. As we pray for other answers on our life's journey, those answers may require more than our words.

When Frederick Douglass, the great abolitionist of the nineteenth century, delivered an address at the Sixteenth Street Baptist Church in New York, he said, "When I was a slave I tried praying for three years. I prayed that God would emancipate me, but it was not till I prayed with my legs that I was emancipated."[3] Uncommon answers to prayer are not exclusively a result of what we do; some miracles come during a time of utter helplessness. But what we do cannot be entirely separated from uncommon answers. James 2:17 says, "Faith by itself isn't enough. Unless it produces good deeds, it is dead and useless."

Everything Means Everything!

Miracles and receiving extraordinary answers to prayer were common occurrences in both the Old and New Testaments of the Bible. God intended for them to be normative today as well.

In Matthew 19, Jesus told the disciples how challenging it can be for a rich person to enter the kingdom of heaven. (The rich young ruler had just walked away sorrowfully when Jesus mentioned selling all his possessions and giving to the poor.) The disciples asked Him, "Then who in the world can be saved?" (verse 25). Jesus answered that, humanly speaking, it was impossible, but with God everything is possible (from verse 26). In Mark 9 He reiterated this truth when He said, "Everything is possible for one who believes" (verse 23 NIV). When Jesus said everything, He meant everything!

Jesus told us that we would experience "greater things." He told the disciples,

> Very truly I tell you, whoever believes in me will do the works I have been doing, and they will do even greater things than these, because I am going to the Father. And I will do whatever you ask in my name, so that the Father may be glorified in the Son. You may ask me for anything in my name, and I will do it.
>
> John 14:12–14 NIV

Greater works are not mystical, or just an idea. It's the reality of what Jesus wants us to walk in. The disciples were told that the Holy Spirit would not come until Jesus had ascended into heaven. When they were filled with the Holy Spirit on the day of Pentecost, the Spirit came to dwell in believers so we would be empowered to do greater works than Jesus did in His earthly ministry. The works of Peter and the other apostles on the day of Pentecost surpassed those of Jesus while He was here on earth. On that day, more were added to the church and became followers of Jesus than during His entire earthly ministry! And the message went forth not just in Judea, Samaria, and Galilee, but to the farthest parts of the world.

Jesus has given us the power to do more in person now than He did during His three years on earth. So why don't we see more miracles, and more extraordinary answers to prayer? Some would say it is because people do not believe. While they aren't wrong, uncommon answers to prayer are also often accompanied by doing uncommon or hard things. In the following chapters are examples.

Are you ready not only to believe but to act? Are you ready to pray with your legs? The combination of believing and acting may be the key to releasing the most extraordinary answer to prayer that you have ever experienced in your life.

At the end of each chapter, you will find five truths that summarize the main takeaways of what you've read. I trust these will highlight key concepts that God wants you to remember. I've also included five questions for reflection and discussion. While I am excited that this book is in your hands as an individual, I encourage you to reach out to others and read it together. The questions can serve as a foundation for engaging group discussion, or thoughtful reflection if you are reading alone. Finally, I've included an action step to help you start putting these truths into action.

—— **UNCOMMON TRUTHS for Uncommon Answers** ——

1. What usually happens is not what *has* to happen.
2. God shows no favoritism. What He does for one person, He longs to do for all. Miracles should not pertain only to the outliers.

3. Uncommon answers aren't uncommon because God wants them to be. They are uncommon because people have decided they will be.

4. One reason uncommon answers are rare is because of a lack of asking.

5. Prayer for salvation and seeking God for a breakthrough are two different things. As we pray for answers in our journeys as believers, receiving those answers may require more than our words.

─── **QUESTIONS** for Reflection and Discussion ───

1. Why do you believe some people have such a hard time believing for an answer to prayer for themselves?

2. Do you pray bold prayers or do you hold back? Why?

3. Have you ever struggled with believing that God does things for those you see as "special" or "important"? Do you still believe this or have you come to truly believe in your heart that God shows no favoritism?

4. Have you ever had an extraordinary answer to prayer?

5. Are you desperate to receive an answer to prayer right now? If you are comfortable in doing so, share it with the group and pray for one another.

─── **ACTION STEP** ───

Habakkuk 2:2 (ESV) says, "Write the vision; make it plain on tablets, so he may run who reads it." Although this was a word from the Lord to Habakkuk, be assured, God wants to give *you* a vision and make it plain as well. What prayer do you envision God answering? He desires that you are able to run with the vision you receive from Him. Get a piece of paper, a notebook, or your iPad. Record the date. Spend some time in prayer, asking God for a vision about how this request will be answered. Write out what you feel He is telling you. This is an important document to refer back to as you see the vision you receive in prayer come to pass.

2

UNCOMMON
LISTENING

Failure to take the time to listen often not only brings a lack of results but also can end up in crisis. Marriages end every day in part due to a lack of listening. Major leadership failures occur due to partners not intently listening to one another. It is estimated that Fortune 500 companies waste approximately seventy-five million dollars a year in meetings due to ineffective listening.[1] Airline tragedies have occurred when planes collided in the air due to a lack of keen listening to what an air traffic controller was saying.[2] Edward Smith, captain of the famous ocean liner the *Titanic*, refused to listen to the warnings of others and continued on, to the demise of 1,517 passengers.[3] In more recent days, the world watched as the tragedy of the OceanGate Titan Submersible unfolded. The CEO of the company, Stockton Rush, ignored repeated warnings about safety and what was likely to happen. "We have heard the baseless cries of 'you are going to kill someone' way too often," he wrote. "I take this as a serious personal insult."[4] Tragically, Rush's unwillingness to listen to the wisdom of others resulted in his demise and the demise of the four passengers who accompanied him on the submarine's final voyage when it imploded.

If you search online for tragedies that have occurred due to a lack of listening, a myriad of examples will appear. It is no wonder that active listening is referred to as a superpower. If this is important in the natural realm, imagine how much more powerful it is in the spiritual realm. It is crucial to listen in marriage, in leadership meetings, or to avert a major public crisis—how much more important is it to listen carefully for God in our everyday lives, in matters big and small?

God Is Still Speaking

There are Christians who believe that God is saying nothing new today and has not spoken since the Canon (the Bible as we know it today) was closed. While the revelation of God's plan of salvation, redemption, and all that He has revealed to us about Himself through Scripture is complete, nothing is Scripture says He does not speak to us personally—giving us guidance, direction, or answers. People who refuse to accept this truth that God is still speaking today are missing out not only on direction and answers but on the greatest adventure of their lives.

God Speaks Through Scripture

We receive information through the written words in the Bible, but also as God illuminates His Word in our hearts.

Many people have shared with me that before they were believers, they would read the Bible but not understand it. Once they accepted Jesus as their Savior, it was as if a whole new realm of understanding opened to them as they read. God speaks to us through His anointed Word, not only through the literal words written on the pages but in how these words relate to our personal lives. For example, you might be reading Mark 11:25 about forgiveness. Suddenly you may have an overwhelming urge to make something right with a person in your life, knowing that you must extend forgiveness to them if you expect God to forgive you. That is God speaking to your heart, from His Word, through the power of the Holy Spirit. It is important to listen for God to speak to you in this way during your times of reading Scripture.

God Speaks Through Nature

Romans 1:20 says,

> For ever since the world was created, people have seen the earth and sky. Through everything God made, they can clearly see his invisible qualities—his eternal power and divine nature. So they have no excuse for not knowing God.

This Scripture strongly indicates that God speaks through nature. It declares that people have no excuse for not knowing God for He has revealed Himself through it if they are paying attention. I cannot even count the number of times God has spoken to me as I have walked outdoors. In fact, it has happened so often that if I need an answer to something and haven't received it, I will often head out for a walk.

God Speaks Through People

Many times God will speak through a person who is sharing something that coincides with Scripture (a word is not of God if it doesn't align with the Bible). One example of God speaking through people is when people receive the word of God from their pastor through a sermon. This could also take place in a counseling session, or at the altar, or during a time of prayer with others. He speaks through the nine supernatural gifts of the Spirit (1 Corinthians 12:1, 7–11). If you have any doubt that God speaks through people, keep in mind that He once spoke through a donkey (Numbers 22:28). He can speak through anyone, whenever and wherever He wants to.

God Speaks Through Worship

Worship creates an atmosphere for God to readily speak to us. When using the word *worship*, I refer to all aspects of our life that are worship to God, including but not limited to song, prayer, fasting, and other spiritual disciplines. Worship is a condition of the heart. When we approach God in humility with gratitude and praise, we catch His attention. The Bible says that God inhabits the praises of His people (Psalm 22:3). When we praise Him, there He is. I have personally noticed that many times when I am worshiping the Lord in song and prayer, whether corporately or privately, He often drops direction and answers into my mind when I'm not thinking about my problems at all but focusing exclusively on Him.

God Speaks Through Circumstances

Circumstances are the facts pertaining to a reality we are facing. For example, perhaps you recently lost your job. The circumstance is that you only have so much time to get another job before money starts getting tight. God will use life situations to put us in position to hear His voice. There is one caveat: Circumstances can be sent by the enemy. We might be facing a God-ordained circumstance, and then again, we may be facing spiritual warfare. (We will unpack spiritual warfare in a later chapter.)

God could be telling someone through a job loss that it is time to pursue the dream they have to start their own business or go into full-time vocational ministry. He may have arranged a job loss because He knew that unless something like this happened, you would have never pursued a new path.

God has always spoken through circumstances. He spoke through circumstances to most of the people in the Bible. An example is in Numbers 22—the story of Balaam, an anointed prophet who had profound weaknesses.

Balaam was on a dangerous course—his heart was not seeking after God, but selfish gain. The Bible records that God sent an angel of the Lord to block his path with a sword. Balaam didn't see the angel, but his donkey did. The donkey swerved to avoid a disaster, then lay down in front of the angel. Balaam flew into a rage and continued to beat the donkey, but received the surprise of his life when God caused the donkey to speak. The truth is that no angel or sword would have been needed in this situation had Balaam been a man after God's heart who sought Him, kept his dark side in check, and spent time listening for God's will in matters.

God will allow seemingly crazy things at times to get our attention. Many times, we believe we are being blocked by enemies when God is allowing an obstacle in our path for a purpose. Sometimes He protects us from what is on the other side. He allows open doors and closed doors alike. These doorways are one of His methods to show us the way to go.

To Whom Does God Speak?

Not only does God speak, but He desires to speak to anyone and everyone. He doesn't wait until people have been Christians for many years. Hearing from God doesn't require a certificate or degree from a Bible college or ministry school. You don't need to be a pastor or hold any particular title. You don't even need to grow up first. Arriving at a certain age is not required to hear from God.

God speaks to men, women, and children of all ages. He spoke to me and called me to serve in ministry when I was seven years old playing in my grandmother's backyard. I have never forgotten that moment. On many difficult days I go back to that moment, and it keeps me going. Just as God spoke to me as a child, from the beginning of time He has spoken to others.

The Story of Samuel

Scripture reveals that Jesus loved children and told His disciples to never forbid them from coming to Him (Matthew 19:14). In the Old Testament, God also spoke to children. Samuel is one example.

> Now the boy Samuel ministered to the LORD before Eli. And the word of the LORD was rare in those days; there was no widespread revelation. And it came to pass at that time, while Eli was lying down in his place, and when his eyes had begun to grow so dim that he could not see, and before the lamp of

God went out in the tabernacle of the LORD where the ark of God was, and while Samuel was lying down, that the LORD called Samuel. And he answered, "Here I am!" So he ran to Eli and said, "Here I am, for you called me."

And he said, "I did not call; lie down again." And he went and lay down.

Then the LORD called yet again, "Samuel!"

So Samuel arose and went to Eli, and said, "Here I am, for you called me." He answered, "I did not call, my son; lie down again." (Now Samuel did not yet know the LORD, nor was the word of the LORD yet revealed to him.)

And the LORD called Samuel again the third time. So, he arose and went to Eli, and said, "Here I am, for you did call me."

Then Eli perceived that the LORD had called the boy. Therefore Eli said to Samuel, "Go, lie down; and it shall be, if He calls you, that you must say, 'Speak, LORD, for Your servant hears.'" So Samuel went and lay down in his place.

Now the LORD came and stood and called as at other times, "Samuel! Samuel!"

And Samuel answered, "Speak, for Your servant hears."

1 Samuel 3:1–10 NKJV

In this passage, we learn that the word of the Lord was rare in those days (verse 1). We see why in the book of Judges, the book that precedes the book of Samuel. Judges reveals a chaotic time in Israel's history, rife with toxicity. The dysfunction of the judges trickled down to the entire nation. Crime abounded on every side—robbery, murder, sexual assault, human trafficking, and more, with corruption running rampant among leadership. (Does any of this sound familiar?)

In the midst of the turmoil, God called a young boy who would be raised up to serve as prophet. Note that Samuel did not yet know the Lord when He called him (verse 7). God didn't reach out to Samuel because they had a close relationship or because the boy had deep spiritual insight. That's important, because it underscores the truth that God reaches out to the unlikely. God is still reaching out to those who may seem unlikely. He is still summoning those who don't know Him yet. When we interact with our own children and grandchildren, and those of our church and community, it is important to keep in mind that we are among those who can hear from God and not only speak forth a word but also change the course of history.

Maybe you feel like an unlikely person for God to speak to today. But He is ready to speak to you, my friend. He wants to speak to you more than you could ever imagine.

One-Sided Relationships Are Not Cool

Imagine a relationship where only one person does the talking. Perhaps you are in a relationship like this with someone. If you are a person who is always listening and is never able to say what is on your mind, you might feel lonely as well as frustrated. You may have even considered ending the relationship. Of course, this is a lot more difficult the closer the person is to you, such as a spouse or family member. Some of the most common complaints marriage and family counselors hear are:

"My spouse just won't listen to me."

"Everything I tell my son goes in one ear and out the other."

"My parents just don't listen or understand."

Relationships are boring when only one person is doing the talking—and that includes your relationship with God. Sometimes it's easy to forget (or some may be unaware) that as Christians, what we have with God is not intended to be a one-way street. God wants to talk to us as much as He wants us to talk to Him. But when many people pray, they consider it a time to tell God everything weighing on their minds, or make requests of Him.

There are many different prayer models and methods that believers are encouraged to use, and these can be helpful. Yet often the majority revolve around how we are going to address God, not how He wants to address us. He very much wants equal, if not more, time to speak to us.

Imagine how God must feel having a one-sided relationship with His children. Although God will not sever a relationship with us due to one-sided communication, it must be incredibly frustrating to have so much to tell us, and little to no opportunity to do it.

What if we are missing the greatest part of a relationship with God because we aren't listening enough?

What if we are stuck because we aren't listening?

What if God is ready to share life-changing information with us, but we simply don't sit still enough to listen?

This can happen, even to pastors.

The Power of Soaking Worship

When I was in my master's degree program, I was part of a cohort comprised of ministers (mostly pastors). The program we were enrolled in was a hybrid of on-campus classes and online. During one of our weeks of on-campus instruction, we were taught by a theology professor who was quite experienced with what is known as *soaking worship*. While this was not part of the actual syllabus for our course, it sparked an interesting conversation. This resulted in the professor telling the class that the next day he would take us through a soaking worship-and-prayer session at the close of class for anyone who desired to stay for an extra hour. The only instruction he gave for those who wanted to participate was to bring a pillow that we would use when lying on the floor during this worship/prayer time.

As we left class that day, I overheard several pastors laughing about this idea and making snide remarks. "He's got another think coming if he thinks I'm bringing a pillow to lie on the floor." I heard another classmate laugh and say, "Exactly, that is the dumbest thing I've ever heard." True to their word, the next day when class ended and the professor told those who were interested in the soaking session to stay, they left—snickering and shaking their heads at those of us who decided to stay.

Our professor invited us to spread out in the room and find a place where we could comfortably lie down on the floor with our heads on the pillow. He turned out the lights and for a moment I honestly did have a flashback to kindergarten where we would get out our little mats for a nap. But that was short-lived. Seconds after the lights were out, we heard worship music through the classroom speakers. It was Julie True.[5] At that time, I had never heard of her. Our professor instructed that we were not to say anything to God during the next hour. We were not to ask Him for anything. We were not to tell Him anything. We were to only lie there and allow Him to "love us and speak to us."

We stayed on the floor for an hour and all was silent except for the worship music. At the conclusion of the hour, our professor turned the lights back on, shut off the music, and invited us to go back to our seats. He said, "Would anyone like to share what this experience was like for you?"

Several of my classmates, many of them pastors who had been serving in ministry for decades, said things like, "I have never felt God's love like that toward me personally." Some classmates wept while they described how the Lord showed His love or spoke to them. As for me, I was absolutely stunned by what took place during that hour.

For weeks I had been struggling with two problems within the ministry that I lead, and I could not find a solution on my own. No matter how much I considered every angle in my brain and prayed about it, I couldn't arrive at the answers. That day, I followed the instructions, not asking God for a thing. I did not bring up these two problems to God. They were not even in my mind as I lay on the floor. But soaking in God's presence, it was if He dropped both solutions into my brain, one after the other. I got up off the floor with answers to the two problems that I had struggled with for weeks. Since that time, I have been keenly aware of the need to be silent before God to receive an answer that may come in no other way.

God Is Not Vague About Listening

The Bible is direct about the importance of listening, specifically about not answering before we listen. Proverbs goes as far as to tell us that to answer before listening is shameful (Proverbs 18:13). It's not in vogue to shame anything in this day and age, but the Word of God says if you answer before you listen—shame! Proverbs assures us that whoever listens to wisdom can dwell securely and can be at ease without fearing the future (Proverbs 1:33). What's not to love about that? We can count on receiving wisdom and understanding when we make our ear attentive to the voice of the Lord (Proverbs 2:6). Answers as well as adventure are right around the corner when we take time to listen.

One Man Who Took What God Said Seriously

Pastor Mike Edds is a man who lives and breathes prayer, hearing from God and acting on whatever he hears. He had a dream in January 1972 of a crowd of people trying to get in the doors of the church he pastored at the time, which was First Assembly of God in Charleston, West Virginia. The dream kept occurring, week after week.

"The church was small," Edds said. "One Sunday, the Sunday school superintendent came to me and said, 'We just can't seem to get more than seventy-five to attend.'" Edds gathered the leadership of the church and shared that he had a dream that a huge crowd would soon be gathered at the church and struggle to get in the front door. The leaders smiled but didn't say much. Edds said he could tell they thought he was just young and crazy. The dream kept recurring, and Edds kept telling the leadership and the church, "We've got to get prepared!" Edds knew that God had been speaking to him with direction for the church through this dream.

Months later, Edds was invited to attend a district training session that was focused on setting up a bus ministry. He left the training with more passion than ever to reach those who did not know Christ. While he was in prayer, God spoke, telling him to take a few of the church's young leaders and go to the most dangerous housing project in the capital city of Charleston, West Virginia, to start the bus ministry. The church board responded by telling Edds, "You've got one month. If nothing comes of this, we're selling the church bus." Edds gently reminded them of the dream of the crowds coming.

In March 1972, he went with a small but passionate group of young people to start the bus ministry. In the natural, they had a reason to be concerned about where they were going. But a boldness from God came upon them as they went from door to door inviting people to ride the bus next Sunday to church. On the following Sunday morning, twenty-six people boarded the bus for church. When Edds and the group pulled up, the doors were locked. He was perplexed. Using his key, he went in alone to ask the leaders why the doors were locked. They told him they knew they weren't ready for what was coming and were scrambling to get more chairs set up in the Sunday school rooms. Edds glanced back to see the new group standing at the doors, waiting to get in, and suddenly it hit him, "This is what I saw in my dream! This is the line of people waiting to get into the church building!" The next Sunday there were forty-four new people in church, and the following Sunday there were seventy-seven. The church grew from seventy-five to nine hundred in one year and became the tenth-fastest-growing Assembly of God church in the nation at the time. God had told Edds in advance, and he listened and was undaunted, even when he got some pushback from the leadership team. Scores of people were saved from that point on. Not a week went by without someone coming to Christ. People were becoming believers so often, leadership began to fill the baptismal tank for every service. As Edds shared his story for me to include in this chapter, he said, "I believe that God is about to do the spectacular again. He wants to pour out His Spirit. Are we listening and acting on what He says?"

—— UNCOMMON TRUTHS for Uncommon Listening ——

1. Active listening is a superpower!
2. Relationships are boring when only one person is talking—and this includes our relationship with God.
3. You will receive answers from listening to God that you can get in no other way.
4. God speaks to people of all ages, backgrounds, and life experiences.
5. You will miss some of the greatest adventures of your life by not taking the time to actively listen for God's voice.

—— QUESTIONS for Reflection and Discussion ——

1. Describe your personal prayer life. Has it mostly been a list of things you talk to God about, or ask Him for? What has your experience been when it comes to listening to God?

2. Imagine that you were given the invitation to participate in a soaking worship-and-prayer session. Would you be comfortable or uncomfortable? If you have already had experience with this before, what was the outcome?

3. Did you ever sense God's voice as a child? If so, what impact did this have on you? Have you witnessed children who sense God has spoken to them about something?

4. The road is not always smooth when we listen to God and want to act on it. Pastor Edds heard from God and received some resistance when he shared what God spoke to him. Have you experienced obstacles when you have heard from God? How did you overcome them?

5. Have you received a solution to a problem as you were silent before the Lord?

--- **ACTION STEP** ---

Dare to have your own personal soaking worship session, utilizing some soaking worship music like that from Julie True. Get in a quiet place, shut out and off all distractions, listen to the music, and allow God to speak to you. Do not say a word to Him. Do not ask for one thing. Simply listen.

3

UNCOMMON WAITING

There has always been a race for information, particularly in the Western world. From 1775 when Benjamin Franklin was declared the first postmaster general to email and text messaging today, the pressure for people to receive immediate answers has not let up.

People in today's society are so impatient for a quick answer, they will do not only inappropriate but annoying things to get answers sooner. Have you ever had someone email or private message you, asking about something that you did not respond to instantly? Sometimes people will resort to posting on your public social media with a message such as "I sent you a private message! I haven't heard back from you yet! Just letting you know!" What pressure will future generations be under to respond, at the pace things are currently going?

Dr. Jason Farman, author of the book *Delayed Response: The Art of Waiting from the Ancient to the Instant World*, shares that speed can stifle innovation and creativity because people don't take the time to think. Farman says, "Almost across the board in Western culture, we see delays and waiting as a disruption to our lives."[1]

It's not just thinking, innovation, or creativity that are impacted by our inability to wait, but the receiving of breakthrough answers to prayer. Scripture is full of encouragement about the importance of waiting. We are promised that the Lord is good to those who wait for Him, and to those who seek His will on matters instead of taking matters into their own hands (Lamentations 3:25). When faced with the temptation to be impatient, we are cautioned to, with the help of God, hold fast and keep waiting for Him to act (Hosea 12:6). With the combination of our fleshly bent toward impatience and culture's emphasis on getting everything at a rapid pace, we often find ourselves becoming frustrated.

How Many Times?

How many times have you groaned when you see the mile-long line at the checkout in the grocery store, even in self-checkout?

How many times have you hit your hand on the steering wheel and muttered complaints when you see that traffic is becoming like a parking lot on the interstate?

How many times have you sighed after realizing you were early for your doctor's appointment, but sat in the waiting room for an hour before your name was called?

Everyday Life Delays . . . What If?

What if God allowed the extensive line at the grocery store because the person with the cart in front or back of you needed a word of hope?

What if traffic was slowed because God wanted to slow *you* down as well, prompt you to turn your music off and listen to Him in the silence of your car? (There have been seasons of my life when my commute was the only significant block of time that I had away from people and responsibilities, and God chose that time to speak profound things to me. He gave me answers to issues I was facing in my everyday life and, at times, more significant answers.)

What if God kept you waiting at the doctor's office because there was someone you were supposed to meet in that waiting room, or before, or after?

What if, by resisting God's detours and delays, you miss out on divine God-moments that will later turn into miracle stories?

When Waiting Is Excruciating

There are times when waiting will not consist of a short delay in everyday circumstances, but a long deferral that feels nearly hopeless. It is crucial to handle these types of waiting periods in the right way because, in this space of time, many people give up or make foolish choices that impact their lives or the lives of others, perpetually.

In Genesis 21, we find the perfect example of how *not* to wait in Abraham's wife, Sarah. God promised that Abraham and Sarah would have a son (Genesis 17 and 18). She and

Abraham were childless and elderly, past the point of child-bearing. To be fair, Sarah was under a tremendous amount of societal pressure. By the cultural standards of the day, a woman's very existence was to fulfill the perceived needs of a man, one of the main ones being to bear sons to carry on the family name. This was more than simply a desire—it was considered a mandatory ingredient of marriage. Wives could be divorced if they did not produce children. That's a lot of pressure, and many women, even in our day and age, have absolutely no control over the outcome. The mores of the day resulted not only in shame toward Sarah but in the assumption that her barrenness was a sign of God's displeasure, even judgment of her.

After ten years of waiting for the promise to be fulfilled, Sarah became desperate and took matters into her own hands. She offered her maid, Hagar, to Abraham, hoping to have children through her and alleviate the shame. What she thought would bring peace brought anything but.

Hagar became pregnant, and tensions became unbearable between her and Sarah. What unfolded reads like something out of a reality show. Sarah blamed Abraham for the situation. Even though she gave Hagar to him, she blamed Abraham that Hagar now despised her. Abraham gave Sarah permission to do whatever she wanted to do to Hagar. When Sarah abused her, she ran away to the desert. An angel appeared to Hagar there, and told her to return to Sarah—but not before he told her of what was to come:

> You are now pregnant and you will give birth to a son. You shall name him Ishmael, for the LORD has heard of your misery. He will be a wild donkey of a man; his hand will be

against everyone and everyone's hand against him, and he will live in hostility toward all his brothers.

Genesis 16:11–12 NIV

Abraham was eighty-six when Hagar gave birth to Ishmael. Years passed and Sarah became pregnant by Abraham and bore a son, exactly as God said would happen. Abraham was one hundred years old and Sarah ninety when Isaac was born. However, the consequences remained of Sarah trying to take matters into her own hands. Once Isaac was weaned, Sarah saw Ishmael mocking him, and demanded that Abraham send Hagar and Ishmael away. She didn't want him to share in the inheritance of her son, Isaac. So Abraham sent them on their way.

Don't Let Impatience Cause You to Birth an Ishmael

You will always regret taking matters into your own hands and birthing an Ishmael. Not only do you have to live with the consequences, but those around you will be forever impacted by your decision as well. It is crazy to think about the fact that this one historical event in Genesis 16—this one terrible decision by Sarah and Abraham—is affecting the entire world today. With the birth of Ishmael came the birth of the enemy of Israel. From Ishmael came the Palestinians and the rise of Islam. World events that have unfolded since that time, and continue to accelerate, are the rise of terrorism, wars in the Middle East, and more. What would have happened if Abraham and Sarah had just waited for the promise of God to come to pass?

There are many times we try to run out ahead of God in life decisions, everything from marriage to children to ministry to career to significant purchases. We walk right into painful consequences that can last a lifetime. We need to keep in mind that delay is better than disaster.

At times, we can also take justice into our own hands, instead of waiting for Him to expose things and set them right. When we try to handle these delicate matters on our own, not only is the exposure of such a thing delayed, but we become entangled in a mess that makes things much worse. While it is difficult to wait, especially amid corruption, it is critical to remember that nothing escapes God's watchful eye. As a friend of mine often says, "God keeps good books, and payday's not always on Friday!" Sometimes, payday may take fourteen or more years.

While Waiting: Sow Where You Want to Reap

Shannon Proctor's dream from the time she was just a little girl was to be a wife and mother. She married Steve Howell in the 1980s and they waited a few years, wanting a bit of time to themselves, as newly married couples often do. But shortly after attempting to conceive, they learned that she had polycystic ovary syndrome. They went to see a fertility specialist and started on what would be a physical and emotional roller-coaster ride over the next fourteen years. There were countless crushing disappointments. Shannon recalls that one of the most frustrating things was having no one around them to whom they could relate. "Steve and I didn't know even one person who struggled with fertility issues," she said. "Everyone who surrounded us in our close circle of friends and our church seemed to be having children left and right."

Shannon was a believer, faithfully serving the Lord. Steve was raised in a Christian home but had distanced himself from his faith at the time, so Shannon was attending church by herself. She prayed fervently both for Steve to surrender to Christ and for them to be able to have a child. As she waited, she sensed the Holy Spirit directing her to do something specific. "I felt directed to sow into the area where I wanted so badly to receive," she said. In response to the Holy Spirit's prompting, Shannon began to serve in the church nursery. She ended up being the leader of the ministry. She also volunteered to serve in children's church and Missionettes, a ministry for girls that the church provided on Wednesday nights. She would come to the church on other days of the week and sanitize the toys in the nursery. At one point, she even took a job as a nanny. Shannon became consumed with ministering to children any way she could.

September 11, 2001, was a memorable day for the Howells for personal reasons. When Shannon's sister called to tell them that the planes had just hit the Twin Towers, they were driving home from what was to be their final failed attempt at fertility treatment. She and Steve looked at each other in shock and disbelief with tears streaming down and said, "Maybe God doesn't want to give us children because of the chaotic state of the world."

Although they would never return for another fertility procedure, Shannon continued to trust the Lord and kept on serving in the children's ministry as she had been doing for fourteen years.

A few weeks later, as the world was still reeling in shock and disbelief, Shannon had a few symptoms that led her to believe she should take another pregnancy test. After hundreds of tests had been negative, this one was positive. She stared at the stick in her hand for a long time, allowing the realization to sink in: She was pregnant, and with no medical intervention. Steve surrendered to Christ and began not only to attend church with Shannon but to serve in the church wherever he could.

The Howells' son Hunter was born in 2002. To their surprise, another son quickly followed. Jonah was born in 2004. Although Shannon had what her doctor referred to as two miracle conceptions, with textbook pregnancies and deliveries, she continued to have other medical problems that the doctor believed necessitated a hysterectomy. On the day that Shannon was preparing to be wheeled into surgery, her doctor came in and said, "Shannon, we won't be able to do surgery today. We just got your pre-op test back. You're pregnant again." They had their third miracle baby, Levi, in 2007.

The Howells thought for certain that their family was now complete. They had a full and wonderful life. They couldn't imagine God blessing them with any more children, and yet that is exactly what happened. Due to a tragic circumstance in their extended family, she and Steve were approached about adopting a baby. In 2007, they adopted Julia Faith, bringing their family of six to completion.

Over the years, Steve and Shannon have been instrumental in ministering to countless couples in the church and in the community. Shannon says, "We spent a lot of time on the ballfield over the years with the kids. Steve and I were a bit older than most of the other parents, which seemed to bring an immediate rapport with the younger parents who looked to us for wisdom and encouragement."

Today, Shannon is still serving in the church nursery where she has been a member all these years—Harvest Church in Lakeland, Florida. Her firstborn son, Hunter, is now the children's pastor. Jonah is in the navy. Levi is a junior in high school, and Julia is a sophomore. All of them love and serve the Lord.

"I knew God was bigger than me," Shannon says. "I knew He was faithful. But I never imagined *four* kids! *One* would have been more amazing than I ever could have envisioned, but He gave me a quadruple portion!"

The Importance of Waiting Well

Waiting has never been my strong suit. My husband gets a bit annoyed at times because I don't want to go to restaurants on Friday or Saturday nights. A wait is almost certain. I'd rather just stay home and eat a peanut butter and jelly sandwich than sit outside a restaurant on a bench waiting for an hour for a text telling us that our table is finally ready.

When I was younger in my faith, I managed to wait, technically, but often would not handle it well when waiting for an answer to prayer. I would rail out against circumstances or consider ways I could hasten the process. Then, during one of my times of solitude with God, He spoke to me. *Deanna, I don't just want you to wait. I want you to learn to wait* well.

Uncommon answers often come not only after a season of waiting that feels excruciating but after waiting well even when things appear hopeless. God has more for us than just the waiting. He wants to form His character in us while we wait.

When embarking on the journey of waiting well, I came to realize that it would not simply be about what people saw me do outwardly, but about what was stirring in my heart while I waited. It was some of the hardest work I would ever do.

Shannon Howell waited well by serving and sowing where she wanted to reap. That is one of the best ways to wait well. Here are an additional fourteen helpful hints to waiting well that I have discovered along the way.

How to Wait Well

- Find hope in God's Word. Find sustenance in Scripture and also in the words you have personally received from God in times of worship, prayer, and other spiritual disciplines. (If you haven't written them down, now might be a good time to start.) Consider those words to be more important than any other words in your life. "I am counting on the LORD; yes, I am counting on him. I have put my hope in his word" (Psalm 130:5).

- Let waiting strengthen you—body, mind, and soul—not weaken you. As the Bible says, be strong and take courage as you wait. You don't have to be a weak, wallowing mess. "Wait patiently for the LORD. Be brave and courageous" (Psalm 27:14).

- Let the time of waiting move you forward in God, not backward. Do not regress into bitterness, envy, or resentment. These choices are a dead end (James 3:14–16).

- Go ahead and soar, but don't try to fly out ahead of God. (Don't birth an Ishmael.) The Bible speaks of

60

"being still" before God. Being still isn't feeling paralyzed or doing nothing; it's resisting the urge to step out to do your own thing and trusting God's timing instead. "Be still, and know that I am God!" (Psalm 46:10).

- While you're waiting, don't get caught up in stewing over the unfair things happening with people around you. Remember, God is keeping score. "Be still before the LORD and wait patiently for him; do not fret when people succeed in their ways, when they carry out their wicked schemes" (Psalm 37:7 NIV).

- Keep foremost in your mind the vision God gave you. Make what God said much louder and visible than anything else you see around you. Put notes up around the house or at work to remind you of what the Lord said. Listen to music that stirs your heart to keep the vision alive. "For still the vision awaits its appointed time; it hastens to the end—it will not lie. If it seems slow, wait for it; it will surely come; it will not delay" (Habakkuk 2:3 ESV).

- There is something to be said (literally in God's Word) about the power of two or three being gathered, and the strength of community (Ecclesiastes 4:9–12). However, remember that more than anyone else's words or practical support, it's God and His Word alone that you lean on as your foundation. "For God alone, O my soul, wait in silence, for my hope is from him" (Psalm 62:5 ESV).

- Remember there are days you will see absolutely no progress in the natural. In fact, on some days you might see terrible regression regarding the situation. When waiting for an extraordinary answer to prayer, it is my experience that the dream has to be dead, or as good as dead, requiring a resurrection miracle of sorts. It's a good thing our God specializes in resurrections. Don't go by what you see. Go by what He says. Keep hoping for what seems to be nowhere in sight. "But if we hope for what we do not see, we eagerly wait for it with perseverance" (Romans 8:25 NKJV).

- Guard yourself against believing the lies of the enemy (Satan). Keep yourself grounded in God's truth. "Lead me by your truth and teach me, for you are the God who saves me. All day long I put my hope in you" (Psalm 25:5).

- It is important not to only serve, but to do so with a joyful heart. "Let's not get tired of doing what is good. At just the right time we will reap a harvest of blessing of we don't give up" (Galatians 6:9).

- Watch out for anger, and don't take your season of waiting out on the people around you. "Refrain from anger, and forsake wrath! Fret not yourself; it tends only to evil. For the evildoers shall be cut off, but those who wait for the LORD shall inherit the land" (Psalm 37:9 ESV).

- Stay steady while you're waiting. Don't give the people around you reason to say, "She went kind of crazy while she was waiting, but in the end it all worked out," or "This wait is making him act like a beast!" There is something to be said for steadiness.

"Blessed is the man who remains steadfast under trial, for when he has stood the test he will receive the crown of life, which God has promised to those who love him" (James 1:12 ESV).

- Remember, no one who waits for God's will is going to ever lose. You are not the one who is going to come out looking crazy in the end for waiting on God. "Yes, no one who waits for you will be shamed. They will be shamed who deal treacherously without cause" (Psalm 25:3 WEB).

- Keep in mind that many people are watching you— even those you are completely unaware of, who will be impacted by you waiting well. When they see the fruition of your miracle, it will draw them to want to know the God you know and follow. "I waited patiently for the LORD; he inclined to me and heard my cry. He drew me up from the pit of destruction, out of the miry bog, and set my feet upon a rock, making my steps secure. He put a new song in my mouth, a song of praise to our God. Many will see and fear and put their trust in the LORD" (Psalm 40:1–3 ESV).

Waiting When It Seems the Dream Is Dead

When I was searching for my father, I came to a point where I assumed the dream of finding him alive was impossible. Just as with Abraham and Sarah, I assumed too much time had gone by. Fifty-six years, to be exact. Emotionally, I prepared myself to find a grave.

During the final years of searching, I was prompted again and again by God to "wait well." I had been helping others receive their uncommon answers to prayer for many years. One day I asked the Lord, "Am I always going to be the proverbial bridesmaid and never the bride?" He answered by asking me a hard question: *Are you willing to sacrifice receiving your miracle so that others might be helped?* I know better than to simply tell God what He wants to hear, so my candid answer was "Let me get back to You on that." Many of my prayers in the meantime went along these lines: "Well, God, even if I were willing, it's just not right. . . ."

God never said it was right or fair. He just asked the question and waited patiently for my answer. It took me a long time, but I was finally able to answer honestly and give Him my *yes*. I didn't feel as if He wanted me to give up searching, only to get my heart to a place where if I needed to sacrifice to be an example to others on how to walk through a long season in the unknown, I would.

I have never waited more than three decades for an answer to prayer. I learned that God teaches us things in excruciating times of waiting that we could not have learned any other way. We can't learn it from a textbook, or a sermon, a counseling or coaching session, or a talk with a friend. Some things can only be learned in a season of waiting.

One of the glorious things about a long-awaited prayer answered is that nothing is a sweeter celebration, and nothing garners people's attention more than a God-honoring moment. When the breakthrough comes, there is nothing like it. But it's not what you thought it would be. For years I told my husband and close friends that when I discovered who my father was (dead or alive), I was going to throw a party for all my family and friends; I was going to rent bounce houses and water slides, and not just for the kids. It was going to be a grand occasion. In my mind, and even on paper, I had planned the party to outdo all parties. But that wasn't the reality that unfolded. When I found Gus, I was immediately thrown into the depths of taking care of the precious man I had found. I didn't have time for bounce houses or water slides. I was doing everything from spoon-feeding him several meals a day to overseeing all of his medical care. I wanted to be with him every second I could for the rest of the life he had left on earth. We had deep conversations for many hours getting to know each other. I never imagined that CBS or *People* magazine, or *Woman's World* or God TV would come calling and I would be fielding media requests as I was holding down a full-time job and caregiving at the same time. Honestly, I couldn't have cared less about throwing a party. I was having the time of my life without one. Once the breakthrough came, it looked nothing like I thought it would. It was a million times better.

When you wait on God, He delivers more than you ever asked, thought, or imagined (Ephesians 3:20).

—— UNCOMMON TRUTHS for Uncommon Waiting ——

1. As you stay alert and ready for God-moments, He will speak to you and lead you not only to receive daily answers to prayer but to be someone else's answer to prayer.

2. It is extremely important to handle waiting periods in the right way because during this time, many people give up or make foolish choices that impact their lives or the lives of others, forever.

3. Delay is better than disaster.

4. It is important not only to wait but to wait well.

5. Waiting is a time for you to be built up in your faith, to learn, serve, and grow.

QUESTIONS for Reflection and Discussion

1. How do you handle unexpected delays in everyday life? Have you sensed the Lord speaking to you about changing your perspective on this?

2. Have you ever "birthed an Ishmael" in your life? If you feel comfortable in doing so, share something about that experience and what you learned from it.

3. When it comes to the ways to wait well, is there one that you feel immediately drawn to work on?

4. What Scripture passage from this chapter spoke to you most regarding waiting?

5. Is there something you are waiting on right now that you feel comfortable sharing with the group as a prayer request?

ACTION STEP

This week, make a point to catch yourself when you are impatient with delays or interruptions. Remind yourself of the importance of waiting on God, so you don't miss out on what could be a divine encounter or an uncommon answer. Consider asking a friend to hold you accountable as you endeavor to be more mindful of this.

4

UNCOMMON CHOICES

Agnes Gonxha Bojaxhiu was born into a middle-class family in Skopje, Macedonia, on August 26, 1910. She was the third and last child born to Nikola and Dranafile Bojaxhiu, grocers in Albania. While her family didn't live a lavish lifestyle, it was a familiar and comfortable one. Agnes could have remained in the lifestyle to which she was accustomed, but at the age of twelve she experienced an inner longing to make a choice for her life that wasn't considered normal. That desire never waned and at eighteen, she left home to join a community of Irish nuns known as the Sisters of Loretto.

While life with the Sisters of Loretto was not akin to what she had experienced in her family of origin, it remained vastly different from the cry of her heart and the focus of her prayers: to help the poor and suffering. She described what she would do next as a "call within a call," or a "second vocation." In 1948 she received permission by the Vatican to leave convent life and launch a new ministry working directly with the poor, called Missionaries of Charity.

Bojaxhiu reached out to orphans, abandoned children, people with leprosy, and the impoverished. She created shelters for the dying, and for the mentally ill. Her efforts were met with extraordinary success, and not only did she establish a thriving local ministry, but satellite missions opened all over the world, reaching millions of people. In 1979 she won the Nobel Peace Prize. Her unparalleled ability to influence by example was evident in 1986 when she convinced President Fidel Castro to allow her to open a mission in Cuba.[1]

Agnes Gonxha Bojaxhiu is known the world over as Mother Teresa. Her desire to reach the poor was fueled by her prayers and answered in an uncommon way, far beyond what she ever envisioned as a twelve-year-old girl when God stirred a passion within her to reach the poor and suffering. However, it did require an uncommon choice on her part—to leave the place of her familiar upbringing to spend her life on behalf of God and others.

One thing that separates people who receive uncommon answers to prayer from those who don't is the uncommon choices they make.

Choices, Choices, So Many Choices

We are faced with choices every day. Some are of greater magnitude than others. Everyday choices include:

- Will I make it to the gym to work out today or not?
- Will I take the time to pack my lunch for work the night before and make the healthy choices I've been wanting to make, or will I just decide to stop and get fast food because I'm too tired to meal prep?
- Will I get off the couch and get a few things done, or scroll through social media and see what other people are doing and talking about?

In addition to the everyday choices we make, all of us will have to make significant choices in our lifetime. More and more in our society, the choices of a godly man or woman are uncommon. But a person who seeks God for supernatural, uncommon answers to prayer will make uncommon choices on a whole different level.

The Woman with an Issue

Consider the biblical story of the woman with the issue of blood (Matthew 9:20–22; Mark 5:24–34; Luke 8:42–48). She had a painful, not to mention embarrassing, choice to make. The issue of blood referenced here was menstrual, customarily translated as hemorrhaging. The cause of the bleeding is not known for certain but could have been any number of conditions affecting females, such as cervical or ovarian cancer, menorrhagia, or a platelet function disorder.[2]

With constant bleeding, it would have been impossible for this woman to have children. In Bible times, if a single woman had an issue like this, she would remain unmarried. Or if she was married, she would quickly find herself divorced—not only because of the issue of blood rendering her unclean but because of her inability to produce children.

She could have awakened that morning, wrapped herself in cloths to contain the bleeding, and made the decision to remain at her home. According to Mosaic law, she had been unclean for the twelve years since the bleeding started. People avoided her in public, quickly moving out of the way to avoid coming into contact with her. In Bible times, people were often shunned when they became ill because it was assumed they had sinned and it was God's way of punishing them. Going outside of her home was a major ordeal. For well over a decade, there would have been no shaking of hands, hugs, or any physical contact to speak of, unless rules were broken to do so. She understood what it was to be marginalized, ostracized, and stigmatized. The heartbreak of her disease was immense. In addition to the physical infirmity, she experienced severe emotional trauma and financial devastation. Mark 5:26 says, "She had suffered a great deal from many doctors, and over the years she had spent everything she had to pay them, but she had gotten no better. In fact, she had gotten worse."

Not only was she bleeding incessantly, but her bank account had bled right down to the last penny. She had to be under almost unbearable stress. The word *suffered* used in Mark 5:26 is derived from the Greek word *paschō*, which indicates not only physical pain and suffering but "to undergo evils."[3] Keep in mind, there were no therapists, no antidepressants, no medications for anxiety, no Christian counselors, no Christian bookstores. She couldn't Google or order a book on Amazon to research her condition or help her through the traumas she was facing. She couldn't have a few girlfriends over to talk about what she was going through. She couldn't summon the older ladies in the village to get their time-tested wisdom. She was deemed unclean; these individuals would not come near her. She couldn't buy anything, prepare food for others, or attend church at the synagogue—not once in twelve years. There was no way to escape the infirmity, or the constant, radical shunning by all of society.

As she gathered herself to push her way through the crowd to simply touch the hem of Jesus's garment, it surely took more than a few deep breaths. It took guts. Serious nerve. She was fighting for her life as she summoned all the courage she had and made a radical choice, so unacceptable for her day and time. And once she made that choice to step outside and enter the crowd, she had to keep moving forward in order to receive. At any point she could have retreated in fear, thinking, *What am I doing?!*

There are many people who say you must be fearless in order to get things done for God, or anything else that is significant in life. Wrong. A lot of people in Scripture who achieved for God felt fear. Moses. David. Peter. The list goes on. They were fearful on occasion, but their apprehension was met with courage. It is notable that people who receive uncommon answers to prayer often possess uncommon courage as well.

The bleeding woman pressed forward, against every cultural norm of the day, out of her comfort zone in every step. She wasn't about to turn back now. She had made her choice, and she was in it to win it.

What might today's woman do?

Meet the Modern-Day Woman with the Issue of Blood

If the woman with the issue of blood existed today, she might decide to scroll through Facebook to see what service she could catch online. It would be so much easier than showering, getting dressed, doing the customary blow-drying, flat-ironing, makeup applying, and driving to church. It would be so much more convenient to lie in bed and watch the service on her phone while sipping her cup of coffee and eating away her sorrows with a bagel slathered with Nutella.

The woman in the Bible made the hard choice. Hard choices get God's attention.

> She came up behind him and touched the edge of his cloak, and immediately her bleeding stopped.
>
> "Who touched me?" Jesus asked.
>
> When they all denied it, Peter said, "Master, the people are crowding and pressing against you."
>
> But Jesus said, "Someone touched me; I know that power has gone out from me."
>
> Luke 8:44–46 NIV

Jesus was not asking the question to condemn her. He was preparing to commend her for her faith. So many times, we focus only on the fact that God knows everything impure that is done in secret and we will answer for it. But just as He knows the evil done in secret, He also knows the faith-filled, pure-hearted acts done in secret, and will respond to those as well. The woman thought she would get away with touching the hem of Jesus's garment without Him noticing, but the Lord is always aware of our comings and goings and the condition of our hearts. When He realized she had reached out in faith, believing, she received more than she ever imagined.

> Then the woman, seeing that she could not go unnoticed, came trembling and fell at his feet. In the presence of all the people, she told why she had touched him and how she had been instantly healed. Then he said to her, "Daughter, your faith has healed you. Go in peace."
>
> Luke 8:47–48 NIV

Notice that when Jesus questioned her, she told Him exactly why she acted as she did. She didn't try to cover anything up. Not that she could have—He knows all. But as human beings, how often do we live as if God doesn't know what we just did, or why? It's always the right thing to do to reach out to Him and pour our hearts out honestly before Him. He rewards that.

Jesus recognized that the woman needed more than physical healing. During the past twelve years, her self-worth had undoubtedly taken a beating. Surely, she felt completely lost—untethered, from her family, from anyone. To this broken and abandoned woman, He spoke life. He went to the core of her identity by calling her daughter. He tenderly claimed her. She was accepted, she was loved, she was family. Then He went a bit further, to address the healing of her spirit and her emotions as He said, "Go in peace." Some Bible scholars believe the instruction to go in peace indicated that she had now received not only physical healing but salvation, bringing wholeness to her, body, mind, and soul.

In seeking uncommon answers to prayer, it is important to recognize that it was Jesus's power that went out from Him and healed her, but it did take effort on her part.

The difficult truth is, people will often say "I had no choice." That's not true. We always have a choice; it's often just a hard one to make. The inconvenient one to make. The extremely uncommon one, especially in our day and age.

The Day Everything Changed

In July 2015, my husband and I were becoming empty nesters and were extremely focused on our ministries—he as a lead pastor, and me as the statewide director of women's ministries for our denomination. We were enjoying a new-found freedom and flexibility. My sister Kim, who lives in the Baltimore area, visited us at our home in Florida. The day she arrived, Larry and I and our daughter Savanna took her to lunch. Shortly after our food arrived, Kim told us, with tears streaming down her face, that barring a miracle of God, we needed to brace ourselves for a funeral.

Kim's daughter, our niece Lexi, a young lady in her early twenties, had been on drugs for five years. The situation was growing more dire each day. Adding to the heartbreak, Lexi had two children: Brody, four, and Olivia (Livvy), one. Through sobs, Kim said, "I've been preparing myself for a dreaded knock on the door from the police, or call from the coroner's office asking me to identify a body."

I said, "We're not going to believe that! We're going to pray!"

"But you've prayed for five years," Kim said. "Nothing has happened. In fact, it's worse than ever!" I could see that my sister was absolutely racked with fear and grief that she was about to lose her daughter. I began to encourage her with examples in Scripture—the woman with the issue of blood, struggling for twelve years; the man in John 5, who had been sick for thirty-eight years.

"Just because it hasn't happened yet doesn't mean it's not going to happen!" I declared.

Staring down at the table, dabbing at her nose with tissues, Kim said, "Well, you're going to have to have enough faith for both of us, because I'm losing faith that this can turn around."

"Done!" I said. "It's game on! Larry and I are going to start fasting!" I explained that some things happen only through the combination of prayer and fasting. (Larry and I had fasted together many times before, and I knew without even asking that he would be all in.)

We added fasting to our prayers, and less than two weeks later, I was sitting at my desk at work on a Thursday afternoon when the phone rang. It was Lexi. As soon as I answered, she said, "Aunt Deanna, I'm going to die unless I get some help."

I agreed and asked her, "Are you ready to turn your life over to the Lord?"

She said, "Yes, I am."

With that settled, I asked, "Are you feeling anything in particular as far as your next step?"

She said, "I've been looking into a thirty-day rehab in California."

I responded, "I've seen people go through thirty-day rehabs twenty times with no change. Would you consider going to a Teen Challenge?"[4] Larry and I had referred many people to Teen Challenge in our years of pastoral ministry, and had witnessed many transformed lives.

"Yes, I would consider that," she answered, "but what about the baby?" Lexi's son had a place to go with his paternal grandmother, but Livvy did not. Taking a deep breath, I said, "If you will go to Teen Challenge for one year and graduate—no dropping out—Uncle Larry and I will take care of the baby."

"I'll do it!" she said.

I had enough experience by that point to know that when someone on drugs decides to get help, you can't wait a week or two to carry out the decision. You have to act immediately—right then and there. After Larry and I discussed the plan, I went into my boss's office and told him the situation. He was gracious and gave me his blessing to go.

Larry and I headed off to Baltimore. Within just a few days, Lexi was in New York, enrolled in the Walter Hoving Home Teen Challenge program, and we were on our way back to Tampa with Livvy. We had only the temporary custody papers, a package of diapers, and three or four outfits. She turned one year old the week we brought her home and took full-time, legal custody of her for the year.

We had nothing set up for her at home, as there was no time before we left. Our home was not babyproof, and we were trusting God to help us to gather everything we needed for her, plus have the fortitude to care for her full-time while juggling our full-time jobs. We created a make-shift bed for Livvy and started to develop a plan to juggle our new responsibilities for the next twelve months. When I returned to work, I was surprised to see my coworkers lined up outside my office door, beaming. Entering the office, I saw diapers stacked from floor to ceiling—about a six-month supply. There was a crib, a changing table, two strollers, a plethora of the most adorable baby clothes and shoes, and so much more. My eyes were filled with tears as I surveyed it all, including balloons, a cake, and other festive party decor. In just a few days' time, my assistant Erika had called churches and women's groups and shared the need. In the next few weeks, our church hosted a second baby shower that provided even more that would help us over the coming year.

During our twelve months with Livvy, she would accompany us to our offices. She traveled thousands of miles with me when I went to speak, stayed overnight in hotels, and became acquainted with thousands of people in churches. Yes, there were hard and exhausting days, but our love for Lexi and her children, our joy at Lexi's progress at the Walter Hoving Home, and the incredible support we received outshone any difficulty.

Hundreds of people would say to Larry and me, "I love watching what you all are doing. But I could never do that." At first, I thought they were referring to the daily rigors of taking care of a baby, especially at midlife. I soon realized that wasn't what most people meant. They quickly explained, "I could never give her back at the end of the year."

It was always in my mind that we would have to return Livvy to Lexi. And I knew it was going to be hard, yet necessary and the right thing to do. I began to consider, "What if literally everyone decided that the choice to help was just too hard?" I thought of all the foster children who go back home after parents get their lives together and are in a place to welcome and take care of them again. What if everyone said no to caring for the children in the meantime?

Lexi flourished at the Walter Hoving Home Teen Challenge, completing her education and quickly becoming a leader among the ladies in the program. We made another uncommon choice when we invited Lexi and the children to live with us as she got back on her feet. They lived with us for five years as we helped Lexi to continue to grow in Christ, parent her children, and become strong enough to leave. Was it always easy? Heavens no. But was it worth it? All day long. Lexi getting clean, and she and the children being introduced to Jesus was worth it all.

Are you prepared to make uncommon choices?

Sometimes, God will grant the answer to a desperate prayer, but it will have to be accompanied by an uncommon choice. This choice may not make sense in the natural. People around you likely won't understand—they may not have experienced a similar choice. Your life may appear to be "crazy" to others, and honestly, it may seem crazy to you too at times. You may have the thought, *What did I just do?* Friends may tell you, "This just isn't what a normal person does." You have to ask yourself, Do I want to be a normal person according to the world's paradigm, or do I want to experience all that God has for me? The two often are not compatible for a person of God.

You may have to juggle multiple things that were not in your life before. Conversely, you may be led to relinquish some things, at least for a season. You may struggle with identifying the right thing to do. God will give you His supernatural peace that does not make sense to the world. Sadly, it won't make sense to many worldly-minded Christians either.

God will open up miraculous doors of opportunity in response to believing prayer, but we must also partner with Him to step up and do a hard thing to see that miracle all the way to its fruition.

UNCOMMON TRUTHS for Uncommon Choices

1. You always have a choice; it's often just a hard one to make. Hard choices are often an ingredient in receiving an uncommon answer to prayer.
2. You will often have to push past inconvenience to receive an uncommon answer to prayer.
3. Being willing to make a hard choice gets God's attention and brings forth uncommon answers to prayer.
4. Pour out your heart to God about your need. He already knows, but just as the woman with the issue of blood spoke the truth when He asked, so it pleases Him to hear you bring the truth of everything about your situation to Him.
5. Fasting is a game changer when it comes to receiving an uncommon answer to prayer.

QUESTIONS for Reflection and Discussion

1. Mother Teresa made the life-altering choice to leave the comforts and familiarity of her upbringing to serve the less fortunate. Her prayer of helping those who suffered most was granted in an uncommon way,

far beyond her wildest dreams. The woman with the issue of blood pressed forward for her uncommon answer to prayer against extreme rejection by society. Have you considered what hard choice God may be calling you to make in tandem with a prayer you are currently praying?

2. The situation with Lexi did not turn around until fasting was added to prayer for her salvation and her deliverance from drugs. Fasting can be a hard choice on its own. Have you ever fasted for an answer to prayer? What was the outcome?

3. When you make a hard choice in connection with a prayer, others may think you have gone crazy. Have you experienced pushback when you have made a hard choice? What was that like, and what wisdom could you share with others about how to navigate that challenge?

4. What makes a choice "hard" may be that it requires us to give something up (time, finances, flexibility, something we deeply desire, having our own way, etc.). Are you currently working through any of these issues in your prayer life as you come to a decision? Consider writing these thoughts out in a prayer journal. Sometimes writing our thoughts to the Lord helps us realize things about a situation that don't come with the spoken word. Also, it is helpful to look back on dates, times, and thoughts about the situation as we give testimony of what God has done.

5. Are you currently praying for something that seems impossible by man's standards?

--- **ACTION STEP** ---

If you have never fasted before, don't feel like you have to jump into the deep end of the pool your first time. Try fasting a meal, or something that you particularly enjoy, such as coffee or desserts, for a day or two.[5]

5

UNCOMMON
SURRENDER

Nelson Mandela spent twenty-seven years in prison in his fight against apartheid, a former policy of segregation and discrimination against the non-white majority in the Republic of South Africa. He was subjected to horrific oppression, including being separated from his family for almost three decades. Freedom for all people in South Africa burned in his soul, and he simply would not give up on seeing the vision of equality become a reality.

In 1990, the apartheid system began to crumble, and Mandela was released from prison. At last, a democratic government became a reality in South Africa. But what now for Mandela? He and his family had been subjected to wounds that few could fathom.

While in prison, Mandela was personally impacted by the influence of Christians. He regularly engaged in Bible reading, community worship, and prayer, and upon his release inspired people worldwide for his choice to surrender any desire for retaliation and forgive his oppressors.[1] He was hailed for his uncommon surrender for the good of a nation.

In 1994, under the newly established democratic system, Mandela was elected the first Black president in the country's history. The focus of his presidency was unity and healing. A new era of peace began. It is astonishing what can happen when we surrender our desires and our lives to God.

What Does God Want?

One of the most powerful questions we can ask is, What does God want? When we wrestle with God, wriggling, twisting, and turning to get the outcome *we* desire, the answer can elude us. It is in surrendering to His will that it often comes.

One of the first things to establish is that God's will is not automatically done. If it were, we would not be instructed to pray the Lord's Prayer that includes asking that God's will be done (Matthew 6:9–13). You can probably think of ten things right off the top of your head that have happened that weren't God's will. As God has granted human beings a free will, many ungodly or unwise decisions take place every day. I personally don't think it was God's will for cinnamon Tic Tacs to go off the market. Banana Nut Cheerios either. But seriously, we know that crime and other evil decisions are not God's will. He works all things together despite occurrences that are not His will. So when people say, "Why should we pray? God's will is always done anyway"—no, it isn't. Prayer can change everything. The important ingredient here is praying that His will be done, and surrendering to whatever that is. Surrender is key and what many people miss. It is one reason that uncommon answers to prayer never come.

Jesus Set the Example

The Lord set the example for us when He prayed the greatest prayer of surrender in history in the Garden of Gethsemane.

> They went to a place called Gethsemane, and Jesus said to his disciples, "Sit here while I pray." He took Peter, James and John along with him, and he began to be deeply distressed and troubled. "My soul is overwhelmed with sorrow to the point of death," he said to them. "Stay here and keep watch." Going a little farther, he fell to the ground and prayed that if possible the hour might pass from him. "Abba, Father," he said, "everything is possible for you. Take this cup from me. Yet not what I will, but what you will."
>
> Mark 14:32–36 NIV

The uncommon answer that followed this prayer was the greatest the world will ever see—the plan of redemption for humankind, accomplished.

What Jesus had to surrender to in that garden prayer was incomprehensible. His agony taking on the sins of the world didn't start on the cross, but at Gethsemane. Jesus agonized so intensely in those moments that He sweat drops of blood (Luke 22:44). This was a medical condition known as hematohidrosis, where blood is emitted through the sweat glands because of intense stress.[2] When considering the story of Jesus's crucifixion, it is a challenge for skeptics to believe that sweating drops of blood really happened, as most people have never seen anything like it. The fact is, although rare, it is a documented medical condition.

Jesus was overwhelmed as He went into the garden and begged His inner circle to stay with Him and pray. They didn't. Not even for an hour. They fell asleep.

Jesus knew what it was to have His closest people abandon Him in His greatest hour of need. Then, even while paying for all of their sins on the cross, He forgave them. All of them, as well as all of us for the times we've failed.

Jesus understands how difficult it can be for us to come to a place of total surrender when we are desperate and believing for an answer to prayer. Even so, it is required. And He gives us the grace to walk it out.

Surrender Before Breakthrough in the Bible

Moses is an example of someone who had a heart of humility and surrender, which was a catalyst to freedom and victory. When God first called him to lead the Israelites out of slavery, Moses was hesitant. He didn't feel worthy of the task and begged God to send someone else. But God told Moses that He would be with him (Exodus 3:12), and Moses eventually surrendered to God's will and led the Israelites out of Egypt.

Esther was an orphan who grew to be a woman of great courage. She surrendered to the possibility of losing her very life if the king did not welcome her (Esther 4:11–16). Her brave move was used by God to free Israel from annihilation.

Jonah was a prophet who was called by God to Nineveh to preach, but he didn't want to go. He didn't like the city of Nineveh—which was Israel's rival—so he resisted the call. While refusing to surrender, he was thrown overboard in the Mediterranean Sea and swallowed by a great fish. In desperation, he repented and cried out to God for help. After God rescued him from the belly of the fish, he obeyed and went to Nineveh to preach. There was a great breakthrough, and the people repented.

Then there was Abraham. God tested Abraham by asking him to sacrifice his beloved son Isaac. Abraham proceeded to show his intention to obey, but was stopped by an angel of the Lord, who said:

> I swear by myself, declares the LORD, that because you have done this and have not withheld your son, your only son, I will surely bless you and make your descendants as numerous as the stars in the sky and as the sand on the seashore. Your descendants will take possession of the cities of their enemies, and through your offspring all nations on earth will be blessed, because you have obeyed me.
>
> Genesis 22:16–18 NIV

God is looking for a surrendered heart. There are times the Lord may not be calling you to do something, He just wants to know if you are willing.

Sometimes we wait for what seems like forever for the answer to prayer. I have learned through my experience and that of others that one of the quickest ways to get an answer from God is to withhold nothing and surrender everything.

A Surrender Prayer Shouted in a Parking Lot

Robyn Wilkerson was a Nordstrom-shopping middle-aged white suburban soccer mom living in the Pacific Northwest when her minister-husband Rich Wilkerson opened a conversation with her about moving to Miami to take on a struggling church. To put it mildly, she was horrified. Not only were the Wilkerson kids happy with Pacific Northwest life, but Robyn's entire extended family lived nearby. They had made the transition over the years from being youth pastors to televangelists with beautiful offices, a large staff, and more. Robyn hated everything about the idea of this move, from having to give up her comfortable lifestyle in Washington to detesting Florida's hot and humid weather.

Robyn agreed to go with Rich to meet the deacon board in Miami but told him she was sure it was going to be a total waste of time. When they landed in Miami, it was as she expected: hot and sticky. She heard foreign languages spoken everywhere that she didn't understand.

The church was located in what she refers to as "the hood." It was completely run-down. Chipped paint and dilapidated buildings surrounded them. Things went from bad to worse as they met with the deacon board shortly after their arrival. Certain rooms and hallways were darker due to missing light bulbs; carpet was so worn, the color was gone; they took a seat on rusty metal folding chairs and shortly thereafter noticed the table they were sitting at was infested with termites.

Every societal ill surrounded the church—drugs, gangs, poverty, violence, and more. As Robyn surveyed the horrible scene, she thought, *There is no way we can bring our children here!* But that's exactly what they did. Rich was convinced it was God's will, Robyn came into agreement with this decision, and they went. On July 24, 1998, the Wilkersons began pastoring Trinity Church of Miami.

The family was thrown into severe culture shock. They were a minority everywhere they went. As Robyn arrived to work at the church office in the morning, the parking lot was already filled with homeless people. Many times, she would have to literally step over them to walk into the office building. Everywhere she turned there were desperate people begging for money and jobs.

The first year of pastoring Trinity almost broke the Wilkersons in every way. In the journey of pastoring their new little flock, they faced gang warfare, domestic violence, and murder of members of the congregation. The first year was filled with funerals. This wasn't what they pictured ministry life being like when they started out. After a year of trying the same suburban strategies, they hit a wall. Money was gone. Ideas were gone. Strength was gone.

At her wits' end one afternoon, Robyn left the church office and began to look around the campus. In an empty parking lot, she looked up to the sky and yelled a prayer. "Father, can You see me? Did You forget that we are here trying to bring healing to this broken community? Can't You send us help?" Immediately, the Holy Spirit spoke to her. *Robyn, are you asking for help to make things look like you? Do you want Me to help you re-create your idea, or do you want Me to help you build My church?*

It brought her to the end of herself. Crying out a prayer of surrender, Robyn was finally ready to live and lead God's way in Miami. On that day, things started to turn around.

Robyn began to see everything differently—from Florida, to the people who lived under the staircases on their property, to the desperate people begging for money. She no longer relied on old methods to try to revive a dying church but sought God daily for His unique plan. Not long after her prayer of surrender, Robyn saw an ad soliciting community agencies to compete for funding for summer day camps. She worked on an application for their church, and they received the funding. Robyn was led by the Holy Spirit to learn grant writing, and she became quite good at it. Through her leadership in this area, Trinity developed partnerships with nonprofit agencies, corporations, banks, schools, universities, businesses, hospitals, and government agencies— federal, state, county, and city. Today, Trinity Church maintains more than 150 partnerships and has acquired more than 100 million dollars in funding for social services for the community. Through these efforts, the church has been entirely refurbished.

Trinity is now thriving. A school was started. Jobs were created within the community through the church. All of the Wilkerson children are now pastoring churches of their own. God has blessed the Wilkersons and Trinity beyond their wildest imaginations. A desperate prayer of surrender in the parking lot of Trinity one hot summer afternoon was what shifted everything.

Fear of Surrender

Have you ever been terrified to surrender something to God? There have been times I have allowed myself to become filled with fear and anxiety over the future—one where my prayer is not answered in the way I want it to be. I begin to imagine worst-case scenarios. *What if I just let go and all my fears come true? What if I fail? What if I look like a fool?* Sometimes these are the thoughts swirling in my head when I first begin to pray, before God starts turning my mind right-side up.

One day as I was bringing all of these thoughts before the Lord, He spoke so gently and clearly to me: *There is no failure in a surrendered life.* It was revolutionary to me. If I let go, if I surrender to whatever He wants, whenever He wants it, however it looks, however it feels, whatever it means, there is no failure. We can't go wrong when we let go and let God have His way.

Perhaps people have told you, "It is what it is" or "Just let it go" regarding your situation. In some cases, letting go is wise and what God wants. But sometimes, not only is it the worst thing you can do, but it's not what God is asking. God doesn't call us to surrender to our circumstances, or "the universe," as some mistakenly believe. He calls us to surrender to *Him*, to His will. People make naive, misguided, or unbiblical statements such as, "Everything happens for a reason," and "Everything is as it is supposed to be." Believing and acting on these falsehoods can leave a person surrendering to the very opposite of what God wants. At times, people claim that they are "letting go and letting God," but that is not the case at all. In some cases it is laziness and a failure to press in and believe God for the answer. Sometimes they are surrendering to what another person wants, which is an unbiblical and unwise choice, or they are giving up because the road God wants them on is not an easy one.

The Day I Flipped the Script on the Serenity Prayer

When I was longing to find my father and sensed it was what God wanted me to do, my mother's adamant refusal included quoting part of the Serenity Prayer. She wanted me to "accept the things I could not change." Instead, I chose to change the things I could not accept. My mother was basing her judgment of what could or could not be changed on her own will. Jesus taught the importance of seeking His Father's will by making it one of the first "asks" in the Lord's Prayer.

> This, then, is how you should pray: "Our Father in heaven, hallowed be your name, your kingdom come, your will be done, on earth as it is in heaven. Give us today our daily bread. And forgive us our debts, as we also have forgiven our debtors. And lead us not into temptation but deliver us from the evil one."
>
> Matthew 6:9–13 NIV

We do not always need to accept the things we cannot change, because there is someone who can change them, and that is God. Through prayer, we can be a part of the process of change. If God communicates that something is not His will, then the matter must be surrendered to Him.

But unless and until that happens, we can and should pray for change and not just let go and accept the way things are.

Sometimes we accept things as they are to have peace with someone. But what about peace with God? We can have peace between ourselves and another individual, but it may be a false peace—not rooted in truth or God's will.

I have discovered that in the process of surrendering to God's way, a thing doesn't have to go exactly my way for it to be the right way. In fact, if you meet someone who believes their way is always the way God will do something, you're meeting an unhealthy and maybe even dangerous person.

As human beings we want to have autonomy and independence and we want things our way. It is the natural bent of every human being to see our way as the right way. As Christians, however, we must surrender our way to God's way in order to find true peace.

We tend to believe that if we have prayed something and God didn't grant our requests, then the wrong thing took place. This is not so. As Isaiah 55:8–9 (AMP) explains:

> "For My thoughts are not your thoughts, nor are your ways My ways," declares the Lord. "For as the heavens are higher than the earth, so are My ways higher than your ways, and My thoughts higher than your thoughts."

When a lot of Christians talk about having faith in God, their thinking is upside down. They say, "I have faith that God is going to____." True faith isn't the belief that God will do exactly what you tell Him to do or not do. True faith is leaving the outcome up to God and trusting Him completely that whatever He decides is what's best for you.

Trust Falls

I was praying through some situations one day when God said to me, *Deanna, I want you to go into a trust fall with Me.* I knew right away what this meant. Trust falls are an exercise in team building that I was familiar with as a leader. A trust fall is an activity where someone falls backward, trusting a member or members of the group to catch them. This was not one of my favorite exercises. I didn't like that I had to face forward, unable to see if the person is really there, arms outstretched to catch me so I didn't fall to the ground. Nevertheless, I have participated in this group exercise.

I knew God was calling me to a life of trust falls, where I wouldn't necessarily be able to see in front of me or have any certainty as to how things would work out. He wanted me to trust that He would catch me as I followed His instruction and surrendered to His will. I'm not the only one—God calls all of us to a life of perpetual trust falls. We are all instructed to trust in the Lord, and resist depending upon our own understanding. We're told to seek His will, not our own, and He will show us what to do (Proverbs 3:5–6). We are promised that if we commit our way to the Lord and trust Him, He will act (Psalm 37:5). We are encouraged to trust God, because that is what will give us peace of mind (Isaiah 26:3).

How is your trust fall exercise going, friend? Are you refusing to face forward—proverbially craning your neck around to try to see what God is doing, afraid that He'll let you fall? Are you refusing to participate in the trust fall altogether, repeatedly taking matters into your own hands, and birthing a few Ishmaels in the process?

The Day a Box from the 1960s Told the Truth

During the many years that I was searching for my father, I asked maternal family members if they had any idea who or where he was. I was always told, "We don't know anything." Usually, people would quickly change the subject. I approached all of the family members I could find and asked them if they knew any tidbit of information at all. Some of them I asked repeatedly. There were several family members I thought might know something more because they were the ones who helped my mother find a place to go when she was pregnant. I was told to never ask again. Some that I contacted on social media initially even blocked me. I wondered why they were so defensive if they knew nothing.

Several days before my father died, I asked him, "Did you think about me through the years?"

"All the time," he said. "All the time. . . ."

"What did you do about it?" I shot back.

"I tried [contacting you], but there were roadblocks. There were roadblocks," he said, his voice sounding a bit desperate. In my heart, I felt he was telling the truth. A few days later, he died.

As Larry and I started sorting through his things, we were struck with how he seemed to have saved even the tiniest scraps of paper. Everything from gum wrappers to phone numbers to bills from decades ago. There were boxes of things from every decade of his ninety-two years. Larry was sorting through a box from the 1960s when he found it. A paper proving that not only did my family know who he was, but he had reached out to them.

People I had suspected knew more than they let on *did* know more. Gus had been truthful with me. He had reached out, and encountered roadblocks. I am not what you would call a conspiracy theorist, but I had been wondering if a conspiracy was keeping us apart, and now it seemed there had been one.

I paced the house, crying and fuming, holding the document in my hand that bore the truth. I swung between tears of anger and tears of joy, realizing that my father cared and he had told the truth. Moments later, I texted a photo of the information to the family members who failed to tell me what they knew. "It was a different time back then," they said. Yes, it was a different time back then, but this was 2023 and I still wasn't told the truth. I felt nothing short of rage.

A week passed and I realized I could not remain in this state of mind and move forward spiritually. It was creating a blockage in my walk with God. I needed to forgive, and I did extend forgiveness to those who had not told the truth.

Why Aren't You Burning Down the World?

As a result of people hearing our story, Gus and I had received several requests for interviews by the media. Those invitations continued after his passing. Shortly after I found the evidence that he had reached out, I was a guest on a secular podcast. When I shared this story of what Larry and I had discovered in the box from the 1960s, the host was dumbfounded and began crying. "This is awful!" she said. "And I just have to ask—why aren't you burning down the world?"

I explained that, first of all, I didn't want to let this situation turn me into a person I didn't want to be. I extended forgiveness not only because it was what the Bible commands but because I didn't want all of the ramifications in my life that unforgiveness brings. I told her I had surrendered to God's timing for the situation. Although I desperately wanted to know my father decades ago, I'm not sure he would have been as open to the gospel then. When I met him, his heart was tender. Not only did he fling open his arms to me, but more importantly, he opened his arms to Jesus. He immediately received Christ as his Savior. If I had met my father decades ago and he had not chosen to become a believer, we would have had some more years together, but that would have been the extent of it. With the way things turned out, I will now get to spend eternity with him. The most important thing was Gus's meeting Jesus. When he died, I took tremendous comfort in the fact that we will spend forever together. I will see him again.

I was able to share with that podcast host what I explained earlier in this chapter. It bears repeating. True faith isn't the belief that God will do exactly what you tell Him to do or not do. True faith is leaving the outcome up to God and trusting Him completely that whatever He decides is what's best for you.

When you surrender, you cannot fail.

—— **UNCOMMON TRUTHS for Uncommon Surrender** ——

1. What does God want? is one of the most powerful questions we can ask.
2. There is no failure in a surrendered life.
3. God doesn't call us to surrender to our circumstances. He calls us to surrender to Him.

4. True faith isn't the belief that God will do exactly what you tell Him to do or not do. True faith is leaving the outcome to God and trusting Him completely that whatever He decides is best for you.

5. God is calling all of us to a life of trust falls.

——— QUESTIONS for Reflection and Discussion ———

1. Is the context of your prayer life more about telling God what you want, or asking Him what He wants? What kind of change, if any, do you sense God calling you to in your prayer time?

2. Was there ever a time when you feared surrendering to God? What was that like? Did you get beyond it? How?

3. What was the most difficult thing you have ever had to surrender to God in prayer?

4. Did this chapter challenge your view on God's will or prayer in any way?

5. What do you feel God wants you to surrender right now in prayer?

——— ACTION STEP ———

Take time this week to write a list of things you need to surrender to God. Your list may include, but not be limited to, surrendering your fears and trusting God more with the people in your life, or surrendering habits you have had in the midst of your circumstances that may be drawing you away from God.

6

UNCOMMON
OBEDIENCE

In 480 BC, King Leonidas I of Sparta had what was considered a small army of 7,000 men who went to battle during the Greco-Persian Wars. The insurmountable task before them was to overcome a massive 300,000-man Persian army led by King Xerxes I.[1] It could be considered a supernatural feat that this meager army would hold off Xerxes's men for several days at the narrow mountain pass of Thermopylae. The sheer numbers forecasted a sure, immediate victory for Xerxes and his men. What was the secret sauce of the Spartans? They were notorious for unparalleled discipline and unwavering obedience to their commanders. Their heroic persistence holding off the Persians during this battle marked a morale shift among the Greeks that helped turn the tide of the war and allow them to mount up in victory. The Battle of Thermopylae is an ideal example of how obedience can change the course of history. When soldiers demonstrate unwavering obedience, awe-inspiring things can happen. It is also true as we walk out our faith in total obedience to Christ, our Commander in Chief, no matter how things appear.

Obedience to God is a fundamental ingredient to receiving an uncommon answer to prayer. In today's culture, obedience to God is often seen as dependent upon conditions, but God's expectation has not changed. As believers, we need to prioritize obedience to God not only as we seek Him for a miracle but also in day-to-day living. Some believe they can live however they want and still receive extraordinary answers to prayer, while others hesitate to obey what God is speaking to them because it is counterculture—it doesn't sound "normal," and they are afraid of being embarrassed.

One of the most basic and important questions a believer must ask oneself is, Am I living in obedience to God? If the answer is anything but yes, this is the first thing that needs to be rectified—not only to hear from God clearly but to obtain the answer they long for. Just as one of the quickest ways to get an answer from God is to withhold nothing and surrender everything, one of the ways to expedite your miracle is to remove every obstacle that is between you and God. You must be prepared to unquestionably obey whatever He tells you to do. Many times, we are our own worst enemy when it comes to receiving an uncommon answer because we are living in willful disobedience.

Just as God is not vague about listening (or much else), there is no ambiguity about obedience. Jesus said,

So why do you keep calling me "Lord, Lord!" when you don't do what I say? I will show you what it's like when someone comes to me, listens to my teaching, and then follows it. It is like a person building a house who digs deep and lays the foundation on solid rock. When the floodwaters rise and break against that house, it stands firm because it is well built. But anyone who hears and doesn't obey is like a person who builds a house right on the ground, without a foundation. When the floods sweep down against that house, it will collapse into a heap of ruins.

Luke 6:46–49

Sometimes, even the teacher refuses to do what their own voice proclaims. I've been that person.

When My Apology Was Eleven Years Late

Years ago, my husband and I agreed that it would be good if I started teaching a new midweek series for our church. I was anticipating all that God would do through this series. I believed we would see many life transformations and have testimonies of what we would experience. I began announcing this expectation in my promotion for the series, telling our church members that great things were in store, and that they should be as faithful as possible to attend services over the coming weeks.

One day I was in prayer, asking the Lord to do all of the incredible things I promoted. I believed this would be in line with His will since surely God desires to do good things in the lives of His people. Imagine my surprise when He told me that an apology over an issue in a church we pastored eleven years ago was hindering my prayers.

A man had been involved in some things that were not right and needed to be restored, but instead of gently restoring, as the Bible instructs in Galatians 6:1, I was harsh. He ended up leaving the church, and it was my fault. From time to time, I had felt bad about that incident, but I thought too much time had passed and it would be best to let it go.

God instructed me not only to apologize to him but how to do it: I was not to mention what he did. I wasn't even to say, "I want to apologize for my part" or "I know I was harsh, but . . ." I have learned that when we follow up with a "but," it means "forget everything I just said." No one hears anything after that, and therefore, nothing is resolved. God instructed me to apologize only for what I did, and let it go at that. I knew this was God because it was the last thing I wanted to do. And Satan sure isn't known for prompting us to ask people for forgiveness. I dreaded it, but knew it was necessary. God strongly impressed on me, *You can go no further spiritually, nor can the church, until you get things right with this man, and thereby, with Me.*

So many times we think we can ignore what God tells us to do, that we can blatantly disobey, move on as if nothing ever happened, and continue to ask God for things. Nope, that's not how it works.

I dialed the man's number with hands shaking. We hadn't spoken in eleven years, and I could hear the surprise in his voice when he realized who I was. I apologized immediately and did not expound. Again, he was shocked. He asked why I was apologizing now. I let him know that I was wrong for how I handled things, God was not pleased, and I did not want anything standing between me and the Lord, or me and anyone else. He was thankful and said that since the incident he had not returned to church anywhere. But now, he thought he might.

Obedience to God is worth it, just for the sake of pleasing Him. The bonuses for me were threefold: My heart was clear, the man was likely returning to church somewhere, and I believe God blessed our church during the Wednesday night series because of this obedience.

The Simple Formula for When You're Stuck

We can't skip steps in our spiritual journey. When people come to me, saying they feel stuck in some aspect of their lives, I tell them, "Go back to the place when you said no to God. Fix that. Obey Him on that matter, and then come back and let's talk again." Many times, a person will discover that their proverbial wheels have been spinning due to disobedience.

The Word of God tells us that if we are willing and obedient, we will eat the good of the land (Isaiah 1:19). Everyone on the planet wants to have good things in their lives, but we often fail to connect the dots about how our obedience to God impacts those blessings. James 1:22–25 says,

> Don't just listen to God's word. You must do what it says. Otherwise, you are only fooling yourselves. For if you listen to the word and don't obey, it is like glancing at your face in a mirror. You see yourself, walk away, and forget what you look like. But if you look carefully into the perfect law that sets you free, and if you do what it says and don't forget what you heard, then God will bless you for doing it.

The formula is: God says this + you do it = blessing in your life. While it is not always that simple, many times it is.

By sharing this simple formula, I am not implying that you can demand that God do whatever you want Him to do. Nor am I implying that you can quote a Scripture verse, do what it says, and expect an immediate blessing. What I am saying is that far too often, we don't realize that our disobedience is an obstacle to moving forward.

Do Whatever He Tells You

In John 2, Jesus was presented with a need at a wedding He attended: The wine ran out. On the surface, this may not have seemed like a big deal. I've attended weddings in America where the beverages have run out, and they simply replaced them with ice water. But at the time of the wedding in Cana, what happened was a major social faux pas. Wine was customary in daily Mediterranean life, but a special occasion took things to another level. Weddings in those days were not just about the bride and groom, but about entire families. Running out of wine would have likely caused a loss of family honor and status.[2] Something had to be done, and quick.

John 2 reveals a powerful exchange:

On the third day a wedding took place at Cana in Galilee. Jesus' mother was there, and Jesus and his disciples had also been invited to the wedding. When the wine was gone, Jesus' mother said to him, "They have no more wine."

"Woman, why do you involve me?" Jesus replied. "My hour has not yet come."

His mother said to the servants, "Do whatever he tells you."

John 2:1–5 NIV

It is crucial to understand that this was the first miracle Jesus performed. Mary didn't know His track record yet when it came to miracles. We know she was not a clueless person. God chose Mary to be the mother of the Savior of the world. Surely, she was resourceful, as many women are. Yet she didn't try to take matters in her own hands. She didn't run ahead and figure out how to produce more wine. She didn't mount up a game plan and send people scurrying to do things to save the day. She went to Jesus and told Him there was a problem.

Mary had no way of knowing what would happen. But when she approached Him, she didn't say, "Now, son, I need You to make more wine." She didn't say, "Okay, Jesus, can You contact Your friend in Cana who probably has a few barrels of wine they could send on over?" Nope. She simply brought the need to Him and let Him figure out what to do about it. To those involved, she gave one instruction: "Do whatever He tells you." That instruction still stands for all of us today.

Oftentimes when we are faced with the need for a miracle, we forget that it's not our job to give God plan A, B, or C for how He could solve the problem. Our role is to listen and obey. Frequently, it is our steps of obedience—to what may seem not only out of the ordinary but potentially embarrassing—that open the way for extraordinarily more than we could ask, think, or imagine.

What Can Happen When You Simply Obey

Trent and Ressie Morgan were the young, newly elected lead pastors of a large church in the center of a rural town in southern Missouri. Faced with the challenge of breathing new life into an older church, as well as seeing the need to update a tired facility, they began to seek the Lord for direction.

One day as Trent was mowing the lawn and praying, God spoke to him about the small, old bank building the church owned that adjoined the church's main parking lot. The building had been purchased by the church prior to the arrival of the Morgans, to prevent a conflict of interest in new ownership and use. The additional parking spaces the property provided were considered an added blessing. Up to that point, the church had been renting the bank building to a local business owner. While in prayer that day, God made it clear to Trent that the church was to sell the bank building. This seemed easy, having been told by the previous leadership that if they were ever to consider selling the building, the current renter/business owner requested first option to purchase it.

Trent called a board meeting and laid out what God had spoken to him. Everyone around the table agreed to move forward. After getting an evaluation of the value of the building from a local realtor, they presented the opportunity to the current renter/business owner, fully expecting it to be a done deal. To the Morgans' surprise, not only did the renter decline the offer, but he stated the evaluation was completely unreasonable and concluded by saying he would be relocated by the end of the month! Imagine having to take this news back to the church board. Not only did the conversation not go as planned, but now an already struggling monthly church budget would lose a desperately needed monthly stream of income. Deflated, the leadership team continued to seek the

Lord, trusting Him with the "now what?" reality of their situation.

Not too many days later, Ressie was at the church talking with the church administrator when her phone rang. It was Trent, asking her to set up a meeting with the local mortgage officer they had used when purchasing their home. Trent shared with them that the Lord had dropped this man's name into his spirit while praying, and all he knew was he needed to talk to him about the bank building, and it was urgent. The office administrator looked at Ressie, and they had the same thought: *This is a huge shot in the dark.*

They discovered that the man was no longer working at the same bank. He had become the president of the credit union at a competitor's branch in a larger, neighboring community. After they found him, an appointment was set. The day of the meeting, Trent, Ressie, and the church administrator met at the church and said a short prayer before Trent headed out, in obedience to what God had spoken to him.

Trent entered the man's office and they engaged in small talk for a few moments before the man said, "What can I do for you?"

Trent said, "I'm really not too sure why I'm here. All I can tell you is that I was praying and the Lord laid you on my heart. I'm not one to play the 'God told me' card, but that is why I'm here."

Trent began to share everything that had happened with the church's bank building property. The man interrupted Trent. "Hold on," he said. He got up from his desk and closed both doors that led out of his office. Then he looked at Trent and said, "Our credit union is looking to expand and tonight our board is meeting to make the final decision as to whether we should expand into your community or another neighboring town. How much are you asking for the building?" Reluctantly, Trent shared the same evaluation that they gave the renter weeks earlier. The man didn't blink an eye. "That's a fair price," he said.

"The church would need parking allowances," Trent said.

"That should be no problem," the man responded.

"The church would also need to have first option to buy the property back should you ever want to sell it," Trent added.

"We can arrange that," the man said.

"As you know," Trent continued, "the bank building is owned by the church, and this means the selling of the building and all the terms will have to be voted on and accepted by the church body."

"That will be no problem," the man concluded. Trent could hardly contain himself as he left the banker's office that day.

Later that evening, Trent received a phone call—the credit union board had unanimously approved the expansion of their business into the church's community, and had completely agreed to the terms of the offer.

That transaction resulted in the church having the financial ability to renovate everything from the parking lots to the main sanctuary. This answer to prayer gave leadership the resources and the encouragement they needed to set a course for growth that launched them into a fresh new season. To this day, Trent and Ressie still lean on the recollection of this uncommon answer (as well as many others they have accumulated over the years) as a result of prayer coupled with obedience.

What would have happened if Pastor Trent had not obeyed the direction, and the sense of urgency, that God had given him?

What Are You Afraid Of?

When it comes to obedience, people often fear the reactions of others more than they do God. Oswald Chambers once said, "The remarkable thing about God is that when you fear God, you fear nothing else, whereas if you do not fear God, you fear everything else."[3] You've got to get to the point where you fear nothing but God. This is one of the keys to an uncommon answer breakthrough.

Many Christians live in anything but extraordinarily more because of the fear of what people think. Whatever you're worried about, remember that it's only embarrassing if you care more about the opinion of people than the opinion of God.

There may be people who read this and think, *Okay, she's trying to turn us all into spiritual kooks.* Nope. That's not what obedience to God is about. Don't take this chapter as a manifesto to run out and say and do in the name of God every crazy thing that comes to the top of your head. What I am saying is this: When you sense something from the Holy Spirit, and it lines up with God's Word, obey the tug at your heart that you have identified over and over again in your life as God speaking. Act on it, in obedience to His prompting.

If you haven't identified God speaking to you yet, there are a few steps you can take. First and foremost, it has to line up with His Word—that's how to know it's Him. Second, ask yourself if it is something Satan would ever prompt someone to do. I can assure you, the enemy is never going to prompt you to do something that will help anyone draw closer to God. The Bible is clear that he only comes to steal, kill, and destroy (John 10:10). Third, if you sense God speaking to you to go in a certain direction that is not specifically mentioned in Scripture, but agrees with it, obey and see what happens. You might wonder, *But what if I get it wrong?* Wouldn't you rather get something wrong trying to obey God with a pure heart than never step out to do what God may be prompting you to do and miss a miracle for yourself or someone else?

Let me tell you about a time when I was required to step out in order for someone else to receive.

A Walk to Remember

I was walking in my neighborhood as I often do, moving along at a fast pace, listening to worship music in my headphones, and praying about all sorts of things. Suddenly I noticed a man in a work uniform passing me on the other side of the street. I heard God tell me, *Cross the street and speak to him what I tell you to say.* I had no idea what I was going to say yet, but having had the experience of the Lord speaking to me in this way many times, I knew in my heart it was the right thing to do. I immediately crossed the street toward the man.

"Excuse me. I know we don't know each other, and you may think this is odd, but as I was walking and saw you, I sensed God give me a message for you." He stared at me, as if he were bracing himself for what was coming. The words then came into my mind. "What you are going through is not hidden," I said. "God sees what you are dealing with in your workplace. Your situation is known to Him. You are seen. And what you are going through, as hard as it is, is not going to destroy you. You are being unjustly treated, but God sent me to you today to tell you that you will make it through, with His help." As I spoke, I could see his face soften. His expression went from shock to almost melting. I went on: "I don't know where you're at with God, or if you know Jesus as your Savior, but I encourage you to surrender all to Him. Turn your life over to Jesus and trust Him. He's got you and your future."

It was not me who needed an uncommon answer that day, but I believe I may have been utilized by God as part of another person's uncommon answer—through a word of knowledge and wisdom (1 Corinthians 12:7–11).

What would have happened if I was off base in what I said to that man? There really would have been no harm. He might have thought, *There's a weird lady in the neighborhood who stops people when they're walking to say kind things that are supposedly from God.* But so what? What that man thinks of me is not important in the grand scheme of things. The real question is, What would have happened if I was on target but did *not* stop? I can think of a list of things, including that a man may have resigned his job before it was time, may have drowned in discouragement, and, as a worst-case scenario, may have not trusted Christ as his Savior, if the words I spoke were any kind of a catalyst for his salvation. In the end, what's important isn't what people think of us, but if we're impacting them for Jesus. That's what we're here for.

Personality Type and Uncommon Obedience

At this point you may be saying, "Well, that's fine for extroverts like her who get high on doing things like crossing the street and talking to strangers, but that is really not my deal."

You might be surprised to learn that I'm an introvert. I've taken every personality test that I'm aware of, and they all come back the same. But of course, it didn't take a test for me to know that. I prefer solitude: reading, writing, and sitting quietly. My calling requires me to lead teams and speak before crowds small and large, and I do it out of obedience to God, not because I get a kick out of being in front of a lot of people. If I went with my natural bent, I would stay at home, or go with a good friend to the corner of a coffee shop for deep conversation. I would not venture away from that table to talk to a stranger if I did not feel compelled by God to do so. And when I'm around people for a while, I need solitude to recharge. If I had my druthers, I'd be sitting at home with my two dogs in my lap, reading.

So, despite whether you're shy or outgoing, an INFJ or an ESTP, a Three or an Eight, a Green or a Red, or anything in between, all of this is for you. Uncommon answers are not just for people of a certain personality type, and neither are the other strategies in this book.

Stop right now, and read this sentence out loud: This is for me. Now, say it again with more confidence: This is for me! Now, do one more thing if you will (actually four more, but who's counting?). I'd like you to say that same phrase again four more times, each time emphasizing a different word.

This is for me.

This *is* for me.

This is *for* me.

This is for *me*.

By now I hope you are getting in your head and your heart one of the most important messages of this book: No matter who you are—*this is for you.*

Being Viewed As a Fool

Obeying God coupled with prayer for an uncommon answer is not about seeking to do outlandish things or taking delight in being seen as a fool. Doing what seems an uncommon thing for the sake of doing an uncommon thing is the wrong motivation. If you are seeking God with a pure heart, however, and sense the Lord leading you and then are viewed as a fool for following it, you are in great company. Paul spoke of this in 1 Corinthians.

> We are fools for Christ, but you are so wise in Christ! We are weak, but you are strong! You are honored, we are dishonored! To this very hour we go hungry and thirsty, we are in rags, we are brutally treated, we are homeless. We work hard with our own hands. When we are cursed, we bless; when we are persecuted, we endure it; when we are slandered, we answer kindly. We have become the scum of the earth, the garbage of the world—right up to this moment.
>
> 1 Corinthians 4:10–13 NIV

Paul and the apostles went through much worse than simply being perceived as fools. They received brutal treatment for following God's direction. Having someone laugh at us or being seen as a fool is insignificant. If you want to experience extraordinarily more in God, you are often going to have to take a step beyond your norm, and move out of your comfort zone. One of my favorite quotes, widely attributed to Adlai Stevenson, is "It's hard to lead a cavalry charge if you think you look funny on a horse." If you want God to do uncommon things in your life, you've got to stop worrying about looking funny.

In the words of Jesus's mom, just "do whatever He tells you."

── UNCOMMON TRUTHS for Uncommon Obedience ──

1. Obedience to God is a fundamental ingredient to receiving an uncommon answer to prayer.
2. As believers, we need to prioritize obedience to God not only as we seek Him for a miracle but also in day-to-day living.
3. Many times, we are our own worst enemy when it comes to receiving an uncommon answer by living in willful disobedience.
4. Often, it is our steps of obedience to what may seem not only out of the ordinary but potentially embarrassing that open up the way for extraordinarily more than we could ask, think, or imagine.
5. Many Christians live in anything but extraordinarily more because of the fear of what people think. Whatever you're worried about, remember that it's only embarrassing if you care what people think more than you care about what God thinks.

———— **QUESTIONS** for Reflection and Discussion ————

1. Have you been faced with a situation where you knew you had to obey God before you would see an answer to prayer? What happened?

2. Have you experienced God telling you to do something but you feared what people would think of you or what the outcome would be?

3. Mary did not give Jesus ideas on how to solve the problem at the wedding in Cana; she simply brought the problem to Him. Do you struggle with wanting to tell God how to solve your problem? Has there been a time when you endeavored to trust Him completely versus instruct Him on how you wanted the problem solved?

4. How might your obedience be part of someone else receiving an uncommon answer to prayer?

5. Breaking free of *What will people think?* is a common issue for many people. How have you dealt with this in your own life?

———— **ACTION STEP** ————

Sometime this week, take at least fifteen minutes in a quiet place to search your heart about anything you may have said no to God about in the past. If something comes to mind, determine to take action on it in the next few days.

7

UNCOMMON SACRIFICE

Monica was born in AD 331 and raised a Christian.[1] Life isn't always ideal, even in a Christian home, and Monica's life took a tragic turn when she was forced into an arranged marriage to a man named Patricius. Not only was Patricius a cheating, abusive alcoholic, but Monica was forced to live with her mother-in-law who was also violent. The marriage produced three children, two boys and a girl—Augustine, Navigius, and Perpetua.

The daily burden that Monica bore seemed physically and emotionally crippling at times, yet she had little choice but to press on. There were no women's shelters, no Al-Anon, Celebrate Recovery, Alcoholics Anonymous, or anger management classes. Looking at the situation through the lens of today, some people might wonder why she didn't leave or divorce Patricius. Separation and divorce were unavailable in her day, even in cases of abuse or infidelity.

Life went on, her children grew up, and Monica worried about her son Augustine. He had completely abandoned everything he had been taught to believe and immersed himself in an immoral lifestyle. Monica considered disowning him, but when God revealed to her in a dream that Augustine would return to faith, she instead turned to two things she believed would bring results: prayer and fasting.

As the years passed, through the power of prayer accompanied by fasting, Monica led not only her husband to Christ but also her mother-in-law. And just as God promised, Augustine returned to the faith of his childhood.

Monica and Augustine are now known as Saint Monica and Saint Augustine. Saint Monica is a timeless example that God honors sacrifice in combination with prayer.

Maybe you are in a similar predicament, where it seems like things are only getting worse. Combining prayer with a sacrifice to God may be what is needed for the breakthrough to occur.

The Day God Sent Down Fire

Scripture demonstrates times when sacrifice makes all the difference for great breakthrough. One such example is Elijah on Mount Carmel, where we see the power of God in response to an actual altar sacrifice offered with great faith by Elijah.

It took place during a low time spiritually for Israel. They were not fully surrendered to God. Elijah invited Israel's wicked King Ahab to a showdown between Baal and God on Mount Carmel, with all of Israel present. When they had gathered, he started by addressing his fellow Israelites: "How long will you waver, hobbling between two opinions? If the LORD is God, follow him! But if Baal is God then follow him!" (1 Kings 18:21). After the prophets of Baal offered their long, useless prayers to Baal for fire to burn up their sacrifice, Elijah stepped up.

He rebuilt the altar of God, placed the sacrifice on the altar, and had it doused with water—four full waterpots, again and again. He was demonstrating that while Baal was powerless with a dry sacrifice, nothing could stop the response of God. He then prayed:

> LORD God of Abraham, Isaac and Israel, let it be known this day that You are God in Israel and I am Your servant, and that I have done all these things at Your word. Hear me, O LORD, hear me, that this people may know that You are the LORD God, and that You have turned their hearts back to You again.
>
> 1 Kings 18:36–37 NKJV

When the fire of the Lord fell, it not only consumed the sacrifice and everything around it but "licked up all the water in the trench" (verse 38). It was a radical turning point for wayward Israel to full surrender. They fell on their faces and proclaimed, "The LORD—he is God! Yes, the LORD—he is God!" (verse 39).

This is the power of a proper sacrifice—even our personal, faith-filled sacrifices of surrender. God sent literal fire from heaven, and He is still sending proverbial fire from heaven today. God sends down fire when our faith is firm and motivation pure.

Cuban Wisdom

Living and ministering in the state of Florida, I have enjoyed many opportunities to make Cuban friends and learn things about their culture. There is a Spanish phrase that Cubans use: *¡Me pica qué, me rasca aquí!* Translated, this means, "It itches me here, but you are scratching me there." This could be applied in several scenarios.

For example, let's say you have begged your wife to stop leaving your gas tank at E when she drives your car, yet she never remembers or takes the time to fill the tank. Leaving for work one morning after she has used your car, you run out of gas. Stranded, you call her to come pick you up and drive you to the service station. She responds with, "Sorry I let the gas go down to nothing—but *surprise*! We are having pork chops for dinner tonight!"

Or you have begged your husband 4,825 times to make a doctor's appointment to get a physical. Lately, he has had some symptoms that concern you. After telling you he would make the appointment by Wednesday, he didn't follow through. When you ask him why, he says, "I didn't make the doctor's appointment, but you'll be happy to know I got us a Costco membership today!"

Or your boss asks you to finish the project you are working on by the close of business on Friday. You fail to do so and when she asks for a report, you say, "I didn't get the project done, but here's a gift certificate to Chick-fil-A!"

¡Me pica qué, me rasca aquí!

The important people in our lives aren't happy when we knowingly and purposely refuse to do what they need us to do and instead offer up something else we believe should make them happy. If these actions don't please our family, friends, or leaders, how much more are they displeasing to God?

When God calls you to sacrifice, you need to give in the way He wants you to give.

The Importance of Pure Motives

Have you taken the time to invite the Lord to weigh your motives?

Scripture shows the importance of pure motives in sacrifice through the account in 1 Samuel 15. Samuel had instructed King Saul that the Lord wanted him to destroy everything in his battle with the Amalekites. But Saul and his army did not; they kept everything that appealed to them (verse 9). When Samuel met them after the battle, Saul greeted him with, "I have carried out the Lord's command!" When confronted with the truth, Saul said, "My troops brought in the best of the sheep, goats, cattle, and plunder to sacrifice to the LORD your God" (verse 21). Samuel responded with this timeless truth: "Has the LORD as great delight in burnt offerings and sacrifices, as in obeying the voice of the LORD? Behold, to obey is better than sacrifice, and to listen than the fat of rams" (verse 22 ESV).

It doesn't matter how hard we work, how great our sacrifice, how much it costs us, if we don't obey God, it means nothing.

Proverbs 16:2 says, "People may be pure in their own eyes, but the LORD examines their motives." God always knows when we're not sincere, but sometimes we don't have enough self-awareness to realize it ourselves. Only through inviting

God into regular introspection of ourselves can we uncover the deeper, improper motivations that could be lurking in our hearts. The psalmist offered up this type of prayer in Psalm 139: "Search me, O God, and know my heart; test me and know my anxious thoughts. Point out anything in me that offends you, and lead me along the path of everlasting life" (verses 23–24).

It takes courage to ask God to reveal things in your life that are offensive to Him. When God speaks anything to you about your motives, deal with it before going on to the next step in prayer and worship. In Romans 12:1 (NIV), Paul instructs believers, "Therefore, I urge you, brothers and sisters, in view of God's mercy, to offer your bodies as a living sacrifice, holy and pleasing to God—this is your true and proper worship." Offering up our bodies includes giving God permission to reveal false motives.

Some Things Will Only Happen This Way

At times, a sacrifice is the missing piece to a miracle breakthrough. In Matthew 17:14–21, Jesus's disciples tried to cast a demon out of a boy and were unsuccessful. When they brought him to Jesus, He immediately rebuked the demon and it came out. The disciples asked Him why they were unsuccessful. Jesus answered:

> Because of your unbelief; for assuredly I say to you, if you have faith as a mustard seed, you can say to this mountain, "Move from here to there," and it will move; and nothing will be impossible for you. However, this kind does not go out except by prayer and fasting.
>
> Matthew 17:20–21 NKJV

Jesus spoke to them about faith, but also underscored the importance of fasting. Some things just aren't going to take place without fasting. I have heard it described that our prayers are like hand grenades launched in the enemy's direction, and fasting kicks it up to an atomic bomb.

Types of Sacrifices

Fasting involves the sacrifice of something you find pleasurable for a season to focus on God and prayer. The types of things a person can sacrifice are limitless, but the Bible teaches that a sacrifice must cost you something. It's not a sacrifice to give up coffee for the month as a fasting choice if you're not really into coffee. It is not a sacrifice to fast breakfast if you usually don't eat breakfast anyway. It doesn't have to be food. I could go days or even months without watching a bit of television. I couldn't care less about it; therefore, it would not be considered a fast for me to give it up. King David said in 2 Samuel 24:24 (NIV), "I will not sacrifice to the LORD my God burnt offerings that cost me nothing."

You may be called to sacrifice your time

There are occasions when time will be required to see an uncommon answer come to fruition—before *and* after an uncommon answer. When we saw the miracle happen with our niece Lexi, my husband and I spent untold hours caring for her children (and still do at the time of this writing). When I found Gus and brought him home, it involved countless hours of caregiving. I wouldn't trade even one of those moments for the world. Friends have often reminded me that although I've completed a lot of education and have several accomplishments to my credit, my legacy will be the fruit borne of these miracles.

You may be called to sacrifice your finances

God will never ask you to give what you don't have, only what you do have. Now, just to be clear regarding the giving of finances for an uncommon answer, I'm definitely *not* referring to a ministry charging you for a prayer for healing, or anything like it. Those types of harmful (and hopefully extremely rare) abusive actions are horrifying and repel people from Christ and the church. When I refer to sacrifice of finances, I'm talking about when God places it on your heart to give, either to an individual in need or to one of His missions. There are many times I have given sacrificially to be a part of someone's uncommon answer to prayer. I have never been sorry for the times I have given, only for the times I haven't. When God is the one who asks you to give, and you do, you will never be sorry.

You will be called to fast

Notice that didn't say you *may* be called to fast. The Bible assumes that fasting is a given. It is an expected spiritual discipline in both the Old and New Testaments. Matthew 6:16 starts with, "When you fast." What if the reason many people do not receive answers is because fasting is not a habit in their lives?

There are fasts that involve going without food and drink for several days or weeks at a time. (Check with your doctor to make sure you do not have physical issues that would impact your ability to fast.) Other types of fasts are partial, which could mean that you would fast a certain meal per day or week, or fast certain foods. There are many times that I have fasted specific food I enjoy, such as desserts, for prolonged periods. One popular fast is the Daniel Fast, where only fruit, vegetables, and water are consumed. (This is referred to as the Daniel Fast because in the Bible, Daniel chose to eat only vegetables and drink only water to honor God while in captivity. See Daniel 1.) If you are interested in learning more, there is an abundance of resources on biblical fasting that could take you deeper into this life-changing spiritual discipline.

Now, let me tell you about how prayer with the sacrifice of fasting brought about one of the greatest miracles of my life.

The Phone Call I Never Imagined

My husband and I have had two wonderful long-term pastorates, but the one before those lasted a mere eight months. Although many people were coming to Christ and growth was happening in every way possible, some of the changes didn't land well with a few key leaders in the church. One leader in particular, Chet,[2] wanted to get rid of us as soon as possible. Chet was extremely influential, in both the church and the community. As life-changing as the services were, everything outside of that became tumultuous. While Chet disliked both my husband and me, one habit he saved for just me was to rarely call me by my actual name. As crazy as it sounds, he had multiple derogatory nicknames for me when he addressed me.

One day my husband was at the altar at the close of service, praying for people, when Chet approached and interrupted him mid-prayer. "Pastor," he said, "when is this chaos going to stop?" This would not be the last time he would interrupt prayer or services with similar derogatory statements. He began to put heavy pressure on the inner circle of leaders to oust us, but my husband and I did our best to hang on.

At the time, we had two children—Dustin, three, and Jordan, two. Although we did all that we could to shield them from the negativity, they could feel it. They witnessed public interactions before and after church with various people, and in several instances, they themselves were treated poorly. All the boys had ever known was an incredibly loving and caring environment in church. They knew the difference between our former church and the current one, even at their tender ages.

At the eight-month mark, things couldn't have gotten worse and the board pushed us to resign. During the days of praying about whether to call for a congregational vote for them to decide whether or not we should stay, Dustin came to Larry and me with tears in his eyes. "Daddy," he said somberly, "the people here don't love us." Larry didn't even know what to say. The truth was, we felt like the larger congregation did love us, and wonderful things were happening. But the inner circle of leaders did not. Our three-year-old son was right.

After Dustin went back into the living room to play, Larry looked at me and said, "I'm resigning Sunday. I can't take a chance that we're going to lose our boys. What will I say to them if we stay at this pastorate, and in years to come, Dustin wants nothing to do with God or the church and says, 'Dad, why did you let us stay in that environment? Why did you allow those people to treat us that way?'" I knew he was right.

On Sunday, Larry and I stood at the pulpit together and resigned. For the first time, we went directly home after the service. We didn't stay to greet anyone. We felt that was best under the circumstances. Soon cars filled our driveway, then trailed down the whole block. People flooded into our home, begging us to stay and take it to a vote, or to consider starting a new church in the community. We felt such love, but we didn't believe it was God's will to divide the church or to start a new one.

We had resigned with nowhere to go. Our bank account had almost nothing in it because some of our income had been withheld to pressure us to leave. We began selling what belongings we could just to survive. We ended up leaving the state and moving in with a family member, the four of us in one bedroom. We didn't have money even for a storage unit. A kind pastor friend who knew of our plight said, "I don't know if this helps, but I have an empty Sunday school room you can use." We were so grateful. The entire remaining contents of our house went into that Sunday school room. The four of us lived out of one suitcase each. Larry got a job waiting tables at Denny's while I cared for the boys. That was life for several months until we received a call to come and candidate for a wonderful church in Maryland, where we would pastor for the next ten years.

Two years into pastoring the church in Maryland, Larry and I and four of our church leaders went to a revival in Pensacola, Florida. We stayed for eight days and witnessed an unprecedented move of God. During one of the prayer meetings, Larry was on one side of the sanctuary and I was on the other when God spoke to each of us. When we came back together, I asked Larry if God had spoken to him. He said, "God told me to go on a forty-day fast for miracles in the church."

"God also told me to go on a forty-day fast!" I said. "This will be perfect—we'll be doing it together!" Larry asked if I was fasting for anything specific.

I said, "Yes, I am. As I was praying, God told me I needed to forgive Chet."

Although God had blessed us with an incredibly loving church, and things couldn't have been better, I was still offended by what Chet did. I believed that due to his influence, my family had nearly lost everything. We had lost our livelihood, some material possessions I loved, and our dignity. We had done nothing immoral or lacking in integrity to cause this—we had only tried to love God, love people, and lead the church into the fullness of God. Kneeling at the altar in Pensacola that day, I prayed, "God, I've tried on my own, and I've failed. I need help to forgive him. . . . I can still hear his awful nicknames for me rolling around in my brain whenever I think of him." I sensed the Lord directing me to fast for forty days, and forgiveness would take place.

Larry and I began our forty-day fast. In answer to Larry's prayer, miracles did happen at the church. About twenty days into my fast, I felt something inside me break, spiritually and emotionally. The Lord replaced the disdain that was in my heart for Chet with love. I felt incredibly free as I began to pray blessings into his life, and honestly wish him well in my heart. I felt so light—it was as if a load of bricks had been lifted off my shoulders. I sensed a new anointing in my life and ministry and was so thankful for all God was doing.

Our forty-day fast was to end on Sunday. At about eight p.m. on day thirty-nine, I was ironing our clothes for church the next day. When the phone rang and I answered, the voice on the other end said, "Deanna, please don't hang up." The caller didn't identify himself right away, but I knew. I could never forget that voice. It was Chet. Adding to the shock was hearing him actually call me Deanna. I could hardly believe my ears—of course I didn't hang up!

"This is Chet, and I'm calling to ask for your forgiveness." I was dumbfounded. I did not go on the fast praying that Chet would contact me, only that God would change me. I almost felt that Chet changing or apologizing would be impossible. But here he was, on the phone, asking for my forgiveness. "I've wrestled with this for a long time," he said.

Chet let me know he was now at a different church. "I don't know if you know anything about this," he went on to say, "but there's a revival taking place in Pensacola, Florida, and my new pastor went there for a while. It has deeply impacted our church. One day sitting in service, I realized I wasn't right with the Lord, and I repented. And then God prompted me to contact you and make things right with you and Pastor Larry. Although I've known for a while that I needed to make this call, over the past few weeks I've felt an incredible urgency that now is the time."

I couldn't believe this was unfolding. It was like a dream. I could not have been happier to tell him that I had already forgiven him, that I loved him, and that I had been praying blessings on him and his family. He was relieved and asked if he could speak to my husband and relay the same things to him.

Only God could have orchestrated that. And I believe with all my heart that the efficacy of prayer combined with fasting accelerated this miracle. Some things will only happen this way.

One more thing. Dustin accepted Jesus at two years old and has never wavered from that commitment. He is now an ordained minister. Larry and I have never regretted the decision to resign, and God worked mightily through all of the circumstances. All things do work together for good to those who love God and are called according to His purpose, as Romans 8:28 tells us.

―――― **UNCOMMON TRUTHS** for Uncommon Sacrifice ――――

1. At times, a sacrifice is the missing piece to a miracle breakthrough.
2. Not only does God ask for full surrender, but there are times He wants a sacrifice.
3. You've got to sacrifice what God actually calls you to sacrifice.
4. For a sacrifice to be accepted by the Lord, it needs to be made with sincerity of heart.
5. Some miracles take place only with the combination of prayer and fasting.

―――― **QUESTIONS** for Reflection and Discussion ――――

1. What has been your personal experience with fasting?
2. What would be the most difficult thing for you to sacrifice as you believe for a miracle answer to prayer?

3. Our prayers are described like hand grenades launched in the enemy's direction, while fasting is akin to an atomic bomb. Have you heard other stories about when fasting had a dramatic effect?

4. What do you think is the biggest obstacle to fasting for most people?

5. Is there a situation in your life now that you feel prompted to fast for?

--- **ACTION STEP** ---

Has God spoken to you through this chapter about fasting for a specific need in your life? If so, spend time in prayer this week to get a sense from God about what type of fast you are to do, and when. Then do it.

8

UNCOMMON TENACITY

"You will never walk again."

These were the words heard by four-year-old Wilma Rudolph and her parents after polio paralyzed her left leg.

Rudolph was born in 1940 in Tennessee to Ed Rudolph, a railroad porter who also did odd jobs, and Blanche Rudolph, who worked six days a week as a housekeeper. Rudolph was the twentieth of twenty-two children, weighing just 4.5 pounds at birth. She had double pneumonia and scarlet fever before contracting polio.

Although the situation appeared hopeless, her parents and siblings refused to accept the bad report they were given. They had a strong work ethic, tenacity, and a belief in the power of prayer. Every night the Rudolph family would gather and pray for Wilma. As an additional labor of love and in hope for a better future, her parents and siblings would often remove her leg brace and massage her leg.

"My doctor told me I would never walk again. My mother told me I would. I believed my mother."[1] When she was six years old, Rudolph began to hop on one leg. By eight years old, she began to move around without her leg brace. When she was eleven years old her mother went outside to find Wilma playing basketball. Wilma developed a great interest in sports and her family encouraged her. She played basketball in high school and was nominated as All-American. She then turned to track and field and was chosen to compete at the college level. At sixteen years old she qualified for the Olympics and received a bronze medal.

Four years later, she returned to the Olympics, broke world records, and brought home three gold medals. She was the first woman in history to win three gold medals in track and field at the same Olympic game. She is hailed as one of the greatest athletes of the twentieth century.

Rudolph's accomplishments did not stop with sports. When she returned home from the Olympics, she refused to participate in the homecoming parade if it was not integrated. She courageously and tenaciously took a stand for that which she believed in, and that parade became the first integrated event in Clarksville's history. She graduated from Tennessee State University and served in the field of education. She continued to help young athletes by mentoring them in local community centers throughout the United States. She developed an organization to mentor up-and-coming amateur track and field stars. During her lifetime she served on many goodwill trips, traveling with Billy Graham and Baptist Christian Athletes. In 1974 she was inducted into the National Track and Field Hall of Fame, and in 1977 her autobiography was the subject of a prime-time television movie.[2]

Wilma Rudolph and her family refused to accept her situation as hopeless, tenaciously pressing on in prayer for what they believed was possible.

Tenacity matters.

There are some things we are never going to see come to fruition unless we refuse to accept the status quo and believe God's Word instead of a bad report. Many times, receiving an uncommon answer to prayer requires hanging on like a hair on a grilled cheese sandwich.

Some believe that people who tenaciously press forward through tough times have some type of special gift—grit, resolve, stubbornness, a stick-to-itiveness—and that they are different from most of the population. While some research shows that tenacity is somewhat genetic, there is also research that indicates it can be coached.[3] This means that however much tenacity you may or may not already have, it can be improved upon. Anyone reading this can become tenacious. But in the spiritual realm, believers are at a special advantage that goes beyond the ability to be coached. Jesus literally refers to what believers have as an "advantage" in Scripture. So take heart, because even if you weren't born tenacious, you can become ferociously so through the advantage God has provided for you.

The Advantage of the Holy Spirit

In John 16, when Jesus was speaking to the disciples after the Last Supper, He said, "Nevertheless I tell you the truth. It is to your advantage that I go away; for if I do not go away, the Helper will not come to you; but if I depart, I will send Him to you" (John 16:7 NKJV). The disciples did not want Jesus to leave, but He explained that it was *to their advantage* that He leave, for the Holy Spirit—or the Helper, as He is also known—would be sent to them. The Helper was not only the advantage the disciples would have but the advantage all believers still have today. And the good news is, that power is available to you right now.

Once believers decide to persevere, the power of the Holy Spirit is often needed to keep that commitment. Tenacious believers lean in. They depend on that power to do what they cannot do themselves. They understand the power of *surrendering* rather than trying harder. It's not that they don't commit and go all in—they do, radically! But they have a keen understanding that their strength comes from the Holy Spirit.

How Would Mary Do It?

When the mother of Jesus was told that she—a teenage virgin—would become pregnant and bear the Son of God, the Bible says that she became "confused and disturbed" (Luke 1:29). Mary tried to figure out what the angel could mean. How was it possible for any of this to be accomplished? She had never heard of such a thing.

Mary's calling would require uncommon tenacity to press through what would undoubtedly bring misunderstanding, gossip, and possibly even the breaking of her engagement to the one she loved, through something that was no fault of her own. She would journey to Bethlehem, and then have difficulty finding a place to deliver her baby. She would give birth to Him in a stable, and later watch Him die on a cross. Most parents do not bury their children—their children bury them. Not only did Mary witness the death of her adult son, but it was after torture and an excruciating crucifixion. Mary said yes to the greatest heartache known to humankind. Fierce tenacity would be required of her.

Are you in a situation where you are also confused and disturbed? Do you wonder how it's all going to work out? Does it seem like resolution is impossible? Perhaps like Mary, you haven't even heard of anyone who has been in your situation before. You are wondering, *Who can I even talk to about this?* You have Googled and discovered nothing. It's okay, help is here. The same person who helped Mary is going to help you.

As Mary considered her situation, Scripture says that she asked the angel, "But how can this happen? I am a virgin" (Luke 1:34).

> The angel replied, "The Holy Spirit will come upon you, and the power of the Most High will overshadow you. So the baby to be born will be holy, and he will be called the Son of God."
>
> Luke 1:35

The angel let her know that the Holy Spirit was going to come upon her and that His power would overshadow her. This power extended beyond the mystery of the conception. The key to Mary's ability to persevere through the unknown was the Holy Spirit.

Leaning into the Holy Spirit is an ingredient most people do not realize is critical to perseverance. The empowerment of the Holy Spirit helps us to move forward when it feels like we can't stand any longer in the natural. The Spirit of God is the secret sauce.

When Mary responded, "I am the Lord's servant. May everything you have said about me come true" (Luke 1:38), she was letting God know, "I am Yours. Do with me as You will." If you haven't already done so, now is the time to surrender your will to God's will. Let Him know you want what He wants—nothing more, nothing less, nothing else. After making this surrender, lean hard into the Holy Spirit's guidance and empowerment. And no matter what you see, no matter what you hear, don't let go.

You Have an Advocate

One of the most difficult feelings in life is of being all alone. Or that you have no one advocating for you. It's so good to know that this is the main function of the Holy Spirit. He never leaves us, He is always for us, and fighting on our behalf. Take comfort today knowing that you have the most powerful person in the world advocating for you, twenty-four seven. You may feel faint, but with your Advocate at your side, you've got this.

In John 14:16, Jesus says that He will ask the Father, who will give an Advocate "who will never leave you." Friends can only stay by your side for so long. A spouse or family member who lives with you is not by your side every second of every day. Even a full-time caregiver, at the least, has to leave your side to use the restroom and shower. But the Holy Ghost is with you every moment of every day, advocating on your behalf. He never leaves your side. This is your superpower in tenaciously moving forward, to not only survive but thrive.

I have met many people who say they are afraid of the Holy Spirit. They fear welcoming Him to come and do what He desires—in their lives or in a Christian gathering. We are often afraid of what we don't know or understand, or that which may contain elements of the unexpected. Fear of the unknown is perhaps the greatest fear. But if people understood who the Holy Spirit is, and what He does, this fear would not exist. There is nothing to fear about the Holy Spirit, the greatest blessing God has given us.

Things to Know About the Holy Spirit

- The Holy Spirit is coequal with God and Jesus as one-third of the Trinity, the Godhead (Matthew 28:19).
- The Holy Spirit is personal, not some mystical force, or an "it" (John 14:15–17, 26; 15:26; 16:7–8, 13–15).
- The Holy Spirit is with you always (John 14:16).
- The Holy Spirit reveals to you the thoughts of God (1 Corinthians 2:10–11).
- The Holy Spirit guides you into truth. He will never steer you wrong or make a mistake (John 16:13).
- The Holy Spirit is your Helper (John 14:26).
- The Holy Spirit gives you power to do what you can't do alone (Romans 8:26).
- The Holy Spirit gives direction for what you should do (John 16:13; Acts 16:6).
- The Holy Spirit is sent for your comfort (John 14:26).
- The Holy Spirit produces the fruit of love, joy, peace, patience, kindness, goodness, faithfulness,

gentleness, and self-control in your life (Galatians 5:22–23).

- The Holy Spirit prays for you when you don't have the strength to pray anymore, and don't have any idea of what to say. When words fail you, He's got you (Romans 8:26–27).
- The Holy Spirit will teach you and remind you of what you need to know (John 14:26).
- The Holy Spirit will never tell you something outside of the will of God or the Bible (John 16:13–14).
- The Holy Spirit will tell you things you could not know or find out any other way (1 Corinthians 2:6–12).
- The Holy Spirit convicts you to do the right thing (John 16:7–8).

Your relationship with the Holy Spirit is the most drama-free, comforting one you will ever experience. He already knows all your whole backstory. He will be the best partner you could ever have. Despite feeling at times as though you can't go on, you can—because of His power.

Jacob's Story: Don't Let Go!

Genesis 32:22–32 records the story of Jacob wrestling with God. Jacob was the son of Isaac and grandson of Abraham. An angel had instructed him in a dream to return to Canaan, the land where he was born. During one part of the journey, he sent his family and servants on ahead and he was alone. That night, a man appeared and wrestled with him until sunrise.

When the man saw that he would not win the match, he touched Jacob's hip and wrenched it out of its socket. Then the man said, "Let me go, for the dawn is breaking!" But Jacob said, "I will not let you go unless you bless me."

Genesis 32:25–26

Notably, Jacob was wrestling with a supernatural being, for no human could simply touch his hip socket and dislocate it. Though the battle was intense, Jacob never gave up. He declared he would not let go until the blessing came. There are a few things from this that we should keep in mind. First of all, the wrestling lasted all night. Sometimes the battle is long! Second, the battle may leave us with a limp, despite the victory that we obtain. That's okay—it shows the world that we've overcome, and they can too. John Wimber, a founding leader of the Vineyard Movement,[4] once said, "Never trust a leader without a limp." There's something powerful about advice or care from someone who has been through a thing (or ten).

Scripture goes on to say that after the wrestling match, the man asked Jacob his name, and Jacob told him.

"Your name will no longer be Jacob," the man responded. "From now on you will be called Israel, because you have fought with God and with men and have won."

"Please tell me your name," Jacob said.

"Why do you want to know my name?" the man replied. Then he blessed Jacob there.

Genesis 32:28–29

Jacob realized two things: that he had been wrestling with God, and that he received his blessing.

There are times we will wrestle with God as we hash things out in prayer and go through the process of understanding His mind and surrendering to His will. It is vitally important that no matter how intense the struggle, you do not let go of God. Keep wrestling. Countless times when going through struggles, I have prayed the same prayer that Jacob prayed: *I won't let go until You bless me.* This is a prayer that honors God. Again, our motives need to be checked. This is not about believing for Porsches or Louis Vuitton bags. This is about saying:

I won't let go until my daughter comes home.

I won't let go until my husband is saved.

I won't let go until my son is delivered from drugs.

I won't let go until my friend is healed.

I won't let go until You open the door for the gospel to be spread to this mission field.

I won't let go until You open the door to the destiny You have called me to.

What are you believing for, friend? Hold on and do not let go. When you think you can't hang on any longer, the Holy Spirit says, *Yes, you can.*

When Grandma Stood All Night on a Bible

In 1980, Mark Purkey was a nineteen-year-old promising athlete and first-year student at Evangel College[5] in Springfield, Missouri. He received multiple awards in three sports and appeared to be the picture of perfect health. But over the year, he developed a nagging cough. During a school break, he went to the doctor in his hometown near Tulsa, Oklahoma, where he received the shattering diagnosis of right hilar and right paratracheal adenopathy with possible lymphoma. He was admitted at Ascension St. John Medical Center in Tulsa as family and friends began to share the news and ask for prayer.

While in the hospital, Mark had difficulty resting and felt as if his chest was on fire. The pain and coughing increased. A doctor came to his bedside with devastating news. Mark had several large black masses of tumors that were dangerously encroaching on his heart, lungs, and trachea. If this was cancer, as the doctor suspected it was, it was spreading like wildfire.

Minnie Cordia Purkey, or Mama Purkey, seventy-five, left a Wednesday night church service in Rogers County, Oklahoma, and arrived home to hear the phone ringing. It was Bill Purkey—her son, and Mark's father. He relayed the news to her about Mark's diagnosis and the need for a miracle. She kept the phone call short, wanting to begin praying as quickly as possible. When she started, she glanced at the clock on the wall—it was eleven p.m. As she called on the name of Jesus, praying Scripture verses that came to her mind, the Holy Spirit spoke to her: *Stand on My Word.* She prayed a bit more intensely, saying, "Father, I come to You in the name of Jesus, standing on Your Word." Again, she sensed the voice of the Holy Spirit saying, *Stand on My Word!* She became louder and more intense in her prayer, and the Holy Spirit interrupted again with the same message, *Stand on My Word!* She didn't entirely know what this meant but decided to take it literally, since she'd heard the voice of the Spirit so insistently. She walked over to the coffee table to get the large family Bible. As she put the Bible down on the floor, it opened to Isaiah 53.

Surely he hath borne our griefs, and carried our sorrows: yet we did esteem him stricken, smitten of God, and afflicted. But he was wounded for our transgressions, he was bruised for our iniquities: the chastisement of our peace was upon him; and with his stripes we are healed.

Isaiah 53:4–5 KJV

She carefully stepped on top of it, and prayed into the night as she stood on God's Word.

Meanwhile, Mark was in his hospital bed, alone and engulfed in fear. Suddenly he heard the large door to his room open. He sensed someone come in but could not see who it was. He was expecting to see his parents at any moment, but no one appeared. Then he felt a very real presence approach one side of his bed. He knew this was the Spirit of God. He sensed the Lord reminding him about a call to ministry he had received as a young boy at Turner Falls camp in Oklahoma. The passion to fulfill that call had gone by the wayside as he had been consumed with success in sports. He realized he had been running from the call to serve the Lord in full-time vocational ministry, and in that moment he repented and surrendered completely to God's plan for his life.

Prior to this, Mark had been cold and shaking, but suddenly it felt as if a warm hand had come to rest right over his heart. His chest no longer hurt, and Mark experienced perfect peace.

When Mama Purkey felt a release to conclude her prayer, she looked up at the clock from where she stood and was shocked to see it was six a.m. She had been standing on the Word of God, praying all night long! She realized she had to quickly shower and get ready to be at the hospital in time for Mark's biopsies.

A small incision would be made first for confirmation of malignancy, then a radical surgery would take place which included breaking his ribs to access the tumors scattered throughout.

Mama Purkey made it to the hospital just in time, still praying without ceasing. She asked to see Mark for just a moment before he was wheeled in for his procedure.

"Did He touch you?" she asked. She didn't need to explain who "He" was.

"Yes, Mama," Mark replied, their hands tightly clasped.

Instead of several masses, only two could be identified. Both were biopsied. When the pathology report came back, it revealed benign tumors—there was absolutely nothing present that was life-threatening. Experts had predicted the worst, but God intervened.

Mark enrolled at Central Bible College in Springfield the following fall. In 1981, he met and married his wife, Susie, who was also at Central following a call to ministry. Since that time, the Purkeys have traveled around the world as full-time evangelists, preaching the gospel and sharing Mark's miracle story with thousands. The story has been shared globally through the media. Some people have reported being healed even as they watched or listened to the testimony.

Are You Willing?

Some miracles are going to require the people of God to stand on His Word to see the breakthrough come to pass. God is looking for people with dogged determination who will honor Him, heed His voice, lean into the power of the Holy Spirit, and tenaciously do whatever it takes for an answer to prayer. Is that you?

UNCOMMON TRUTHS for Uncommon Tenacity

1. There are some things we are never going to see come to fruition unless we refuse to accept the status quo and believe God's Word over the bad report that we have been given.

2. Many times, receiving an uncommon answer to prayer requires hanging on like a hair on a grilled cheese sandwich.

3. Tenacious believers lean into the power of the Holy Spirit to do what they cannot do themselves.

4. The Holy Spirit is with you every moment of every day, advocating on your behalf. He never leaves your side. This is your superpower in persistently moving forward, to not only survive but thrive.

5. There are times we will wrestle with God as we hash things out in prayer and go through the process of understanding His mind and surrendering to His will.

QUESTIONS for Reflection and Discussion

1. What is your typical response when you receive a bad report of some kind? Do you sense God speaking to you to adjust your response in any way?

2. What has your experience been with the Holy Spirit? What opinions have you held about Him that you realized later were not accurate?

3. Have you been tempted in the past to believe that some people simply have a gift of tenacity? Do you still feel that way?

4. Does knowing that the Holy Spirit is your twenty-four seven Advocate, or the best Friend you will ever have, bring comfort to you? How could the reality of His abiding presence change things for you on a daily basis?

5. What prayer request are you tenaciously believing for, not letting go until God brings the answer?

ACTION STEP

Is there a prayer request you have been tempted to give up on, or in fact *have* given up on? Maybe you have been praying for a long time with no change, and deep down you believe it's either not God's will or is too hard for Him. If so, recommit it to prayer right now. Say out loud, "I won't let go until [fill in the blank with your prayer request] is answered."

9

UNCOMMON
RIGHTEOUSNESS

Medgar Evers, a Black man from Mississippi, worked as a
traveling insurance salesperson in the 1960s. In his travels,
he became increasingly aware of the plight of Black Americans. He was compelled to do something to bring equality
and a better future. He became active in civil rights work
and served tirelessly to see desegregation become a reality.
Unfortunately, he quickly became a target for militant white
supremacists. In the wee hours of June 12, 1963, he was
gunned down in his driveway and died in front of his two
small children.[1] His grief-stricken widow, Myrlie Evers, fervently prayed for justice.

The suspect in Evers's murder was white supremacist
Byron de la Beckwith. All of the evidence against De la
Beckwith was present, including the gun with his fresh fin-
gerprints on it. But two white police officers quickly came

forward to claim they had seen him in Greenwood, Mississippi, at the time of the crime, which was sixty miles from Evers's home.

De la Beckwith was arrested and tried for Evers's murder, twice, but both trials ended with hung juries. In 1994, however, new evidence was brought to light, including six witnesses who testified that they heard De la Beckwith brag about killing Evers. He was retried and received a life sentence in prison. When the judge pronounced the sentence, Myrlie's reaction was reported.

> "All I want to say is, "Yay, Medgar, yay!" She wiped away tears. "My God! I don't have to say accused assassin anymore. I can say convicted assassin, who laughed and said, 'He's dead, isn't he? That's one n—— who isn't going to come back.' But what he failed to realize was that Medgar was still alive in spirit and through each and every one of us who wanted to see justice done."[2]

Myrlie's prayers were not in vain, and although it took thirty-one years to receive her answer, it was received. Byron de la Beckwith remained in prison until he died in 2001. Evers's story of justice delayed but not denied is portrayed in the soul-stirring movie *Ghosts of Mississippi*.

Praying for Wrong to Be Righted

Waiting in prayer for wrongs to be exposed or justice to be served can feel excruciating. It can be brutal whether you are waiting for exoneration, having been falsely accused, or waiting for someone else to bear the consequences of their wrong. To receive an uncommon answer to prayer, particularly regarding a wrong you or someone else has experienced, an uncommon righteousness will be required. As Paul advised Timothy, "Keep your head in all situations, endure hardship" (2 Timothy 4:5 NIV). Above all, remember that it's never the right time to do the wrong thing.

Pain on All Levels

Perhaps you are not in the situation of Myrlie Evers, but your pain is just as real. The cry of your heart for justice is ever-present. Injustice and corruption can be found on many distinct levels. You may face unjust circumstances, dirty politics, and corruption in both the world and the church. Perhaps you are reeling from the infidelity of a spouse, betrayal from an extended family member, or church hurt. You might be aware of corruption that no one else sees or, in your opinion, would ever believe. Some people, even when presented with hard cold evidence, still will not accept the facts. I truly believe that Jesus Christ Himself could walk up to some people and tell them the truth about these types of things and they still would not receive it.

In the Christian community the pain is often worse because we expect so much more. We expect our Christian spouse to be different. We expect our Christian extended family member to be different. We expect our Christian boss to be different. And when they are not, it can bring severe disillusionment that few understand.

As I ascended in leadership from the local church to city/regional and then statewide, I naively assumed that I would run into fewer situations of corruption. Instead, I became privy to more. I quickly came to realize why Paul warned Timothy against giving church leadership to a recent convert (in 1 Timothy 3:6). The higher you go in leadership, the more integrity, grace, and wisdom it takes to navigate circumstances in righteousness.

Stay on God's Side

One day I was sick and tired of being sick and tired. I was laden down with cares about things swirling around me that I knew weren't right, but felt powerless to do anything about them. I began to cry out to God, *I need You on my side, God! I need You on my side!* The Holy Spirit gently interrupted that prayer and said, *Why don't you get on My side?*

Oof.

After the Holy Spirit said it, it seemed so simple, I didn't know how I missed it. I realized that, depending on the situation, He might be on my side, or He might not be. God supporting me on a particular issue could change from day to day and situation to situation, depending on whether I was right or wrong (and I'm wrong plenty of times). But if I would just get on His side, I would always win. Because God never loses.

How do we get on God's side? By doing things God's way.

We get on God's side by responding as Jesus would in every situation.

We get on God's side by living righteously.

We get on God's side by living and acting in integrity.

If someone lashes out with hate, we respond with love. If someone stirs up strife, we respond with peace. If someone refuses to forgive, we forgive anyway. If someone talks trash about us, we cast the trash that was spoken aside, and keep on loving.

I was trying my best to do these things; I just needed to turn the focus off myself.

Some leaders mistakenly believe that God is on their side simply because they hold a title or a leadership position. Perhaps they misguidedly think that God is always on their side because He allowed them to be there. They believe God appointed them, or allowed them to be elected, so surely His blessing is upon them.

God's Word instructs people to honor their leaders, but does He always agree with, endorse, or bless what those leaders do? No. God's hand is not on leaders simply because they are the leaders. Believe me, I live with the reality that God's hand on me as a leader is not automatic. A righteous life does not come without intentionality. A person can become so desensitized that they don't even know they no longer have God's approval. I don't want to be that person. It has been sobering for me to see so many of my leader-friends with their lives and ministries now in shambles.

God is not on your side simply because you are the pastor, director, bishop, CEO, executive, overseer, or superintendent, regardless of your denomination. God will not grant an uncommon answer to prayer based on position or title.

God Is on the Side of the Righteous

Righteousness is being right with God and doing things God's way. We learn about God's ways through reading God's Word. Righteousness is so important to God, He values it more than anything we could ever sacrifice (Proverbs

21:3). The Bible says that God is listening to the righteous. "The eyes of the LORD watch over those who do right; his ears are open to their cries for help" (Psalm 34:15), but "The Lord turns his face against those who do evil" (1 Peter 3:12). As you walk in righteousness, you can be sure God's ears are open to you and His eyes are on you. What a comfort.

When dealing with those who are acting unrighteously, we may be tempted to fear what will happen to us, our loved ones, our livelihood, our home, our job, our ministry, or more. These fears are common. Yet consider Proverbs 13:6, "Righteousness guards him whose way is blameless, but sin overthrows the wicked" (ESV). This doesn't mean we won't go through a difficulty or two (or ten), but that ultimately, God will guard the righteous and overthrow the wicked. You may have to wait a significant period of time to see "extraordinarily more" in this regard, but for the righteous, it is a principle in Scripture that can be counted on.

The Bible is specific about the type of person whose prayers garner God's attention. "The earnest prayer of a righteous person has great power and produces wonderful results" (James 5:16). James also indicates there is a harvest that we can expect as a result of righteousness (3:18). If we want to have great power in our prayers and produce wonderful results, righteousness is nonnegotiable.

Blessing Follows Righteousness

When we respond righteously, blessings follow. "Blessed are they who observe justice, who do righteousness at all times!" (Psalm 106:3 ESV). Although we are guaranteed to prevail in living righteously, there are many moments along the way when we feel as if we cannot take it a moment longer. Scripture says you will be provided for.

> He who walks righteously and speaks uprightly, who despises the gain of oppressions, who shakes his hands, lest they hold a bribe, who stops his ears from hearing of bloodshed and shuts his eyes from looking on evil, he will dwell on the heights; his place of defense will be the fortresses of rocks; his bread will be given him; his water will be sure.
>
> Isaiah 33:15–17 ESV

We are given the instruction that as we seek first the kingdom of God and His righteousness, all these things will be added to us (Matthew 6:33). The kingdom of God is all about *His* way to receive all the good things.

There are times you may go through situations that are bizarre and deplorable as you wait for your uncommon answer to prayer. Such was the case of Rhonda Kenner.

Standing Upright When Wronged

Rhonda Kenner[3] was known as one of the greatest ministry leaders in the area of youth and young adults, not only in her church and region but across the United States. She had a track record of developing some of the strongest young leaders in her denomination and beyond. Her longest tenure at one church was seventeen years, with an impeccable record. Under Rhonda's leadership the youth department had exploded to where she was leading six full-time staff and three interns. Then, in year sixteen, something shifted.

Rhonda began receiving strange texts from the lead pastor. The texts began as casual communication but became sexually explicit. Rhonda was a devoted wife and mother and had done nothing to encourage this communication. Each time she received one, she immediately showed it to her husband, who was equally mortified. Rhonda would respond every time, indicating that the texts were inappropriate and needed to stop. Unfortunately, they did not stop. When Rhonda started to ignore the pastor's texts of this nature, she was called into his office and told, "I am your boss. You will respond to all of my communication."

Rhonda and her husband attempted to handle the problem through the appropriate channels. But unfortunately, some leaders manage to insulate themselves from all accountability. It was a setting that could be described as cult-like. Everyone in the church, especially leadership, had been conditioned to be loyal to the lead pastor at all costs—they were trained to refuse any negative word concerning the pastor. No one would hear Rhonda's concern.

One day, after the pastor made an inappropriate comment to her in person, Rhonda went into her office, collapsed on the floor, and cried, "Lord, I can't do this anymore!" She resigned that day. When Rhonda reached out to the state overseer to share her concerns, it went nowhere. He and the pastor had been close friends for thirty-five years.

When Rhonda's phone was broken into in an effort to erase the evidence of the texts sent by the pastor, she consulted an attorney. She was informed that what had been committed by the pastor and those who helped him break into her phone was a federal crime. The attorney recommended that she sue not only the pastor but the church and the denomination. She was assured that with all the evidence that was mounting, she would receive a lucrative settlement and the church would more than likely shut down under the weight of what was sure to be a settlement that would financially crush them. Rhonda did not feel comfortable suing the church and the denomination. But on her attorney's advice, she supplied written documentation to expose the situation.

Rhonda prayed for a peaceful resolution. She describes what happened next as like a bomb hitting the church and community. With the overwhelming evidence of the pastor's sexual harassment in the hands of a substantial number of local and state denominational officials, something had to be done. The pastor was removed from office and placed within the denomination's restoration program.

With the truth out in the open, Rhonda expected that board members and elders who had previously refused to talk to her would come running with their apologies and condolences. Instead, they responded in the opposite spirit. Almost everyone was angry with Rhonda for what they perceived as her wrecking their church.

Rhonda was well known for her work with youth and had ministry job offers coming in, big offers with a generous salary package and benefits. She could have stayed in the same geographical area, acquired a new ministry position, and tried to defend herself against the accusations that she had ruined the church. Instead, she made the decision to move forward peacefully and prayerfully.

Despite having even non-ministry job offers that might have seemed like a smarter choice, Rhonda felt directed to accept an offer from a much smaller church that had contacted her from eight hundred miles away. This would mean leaving their entire extended family and support system to go to a tiny town most people had never heard of. The salary package at the new church was an $18,000 pay cut, in addition to having to raise all of the funds needed to hire future staff and provide for the needs of the ministry. Nevertheless, at God's beckoning, the Kenners packed their U-Haul and headed west.

God blessed Rhonda's ministry once again as she raised another discipleship program from scratch that became (and is still known as) one of the best in the country. Despite the upheaval that happened in the previous church, all of Rhonda's children are Christians today. She thrived in the years following her traumatic experience, and she continues to thrive, investing in and raising up ministry leaders. The pastor who sexually harassed Rhonda dropped out of the restoration program after six months, never returned to ministry, and has endured many heartaches since. Almost all of the deacons and elders who turned a deaf ear to Rhonda's cries for help have also faced tremendous hardships. We can learn a lot by the outcome of this situation, seeing it from beginning to end. It is good to remember that "the LORD is a God of justice; blessed are all those who wait for him" (Isaiah 30:18 ESV).

Just Pain—or God's Protection?

Sometimes we see ungodly leaders get away with wrongdoing for a lengthy period of time and we think to ourselves, *Surely God can't work through them because they are so corrupt!* You would be surprised at who and what God can use.

One day Larry and I were working out in our yard, when Larry put his hand in a hole and immediately was bitten by a fire ant. He jerked his hand out and began shaking it in pain. If you live in the South, you likely know just how painful this can be. Larry was still complaining about the ant bite when suddenly, a venomous cottonmouth snake reared its head out of the same hole! Larry jumped back quickly. Never were the two of us so grateful for a fire ant. If Larry hadn't jerked his hand out of that hole, he likely would have been bitten by the snake.

There are times God will send a fire ant to save you from a snake. I have learned that even egregious situations contain hidden treasures. God can use your tough situation to protect you from a colossal tragedy; He can also use it to catapult you into your destiny.

One of my favorite Scripture verses is "I will give you treasures hidden in the darkness—secret riches. I will do this so you may know that I am the LORD, the God of Israel, the one who calls you by name" (Isaiah 45:3). I went back to this verse again and again for years because it reminded me that in the dark times, God would give me special treasures that I could receive in no other way. This Scripture comforted me. Later, I discovered a deeper meaning to this verse as I was studying. In this passage, Isaiah refers to King Cyrus as the Lord's shepherd (Isaiah 44:28), and the Lord's anointed (Isaiah 45:1). He was chosen to set up the divine plan of setting Israel free from captivity, yet Cyrus did not know Jehovah. There are times when God allows unrighteous people to be elected or appointed in both sacred and secular circles for His purposes. Cyrus became a tool in the hands of God about 150 years after Isaiah's prophecy—which means that Isaiah called Cyrus by name (in Isaiah 45:1) almost 150 years before he ruled! Although Cyrus did not know the Lord or obey Him, God chose to use him. Despite what things looked like from the outside, God was in control.

God can use a donkey.

God can use a fire ant.

God can use an atheist.

God can use your unbelieving spouse.

God can use a religious leader who is only posing as a believer.

God can use that person at work who is getting on your last nerve.

God can and often does use the person or thing you least expect.

God can use anyone as His tool to accomplish His will. He holds power over all things—even things and people who seem out of control. While they are out of *our* control, they are not out of God's. He can use even them to get you where you need to go.

Things Aren't Always As They Seem

As you're waiting for your prayer to be answered, keep in mind that what happened to Daniel regarding his delayed answer to prayer is often our reality. After Daniel had prayed and fasted for twenty-one days, an angel was sent to him by God with a message of encouragement about the delay.

Don't be afraid, Daniel. Since the first day you began to pray for understanding and to humble yourself before your God, your request has been heard in heaven. I have come in answer to your prayer. But for twenty-one days the spirit prince of the kingdom of Persia blocked my way. Then Michael, one of the archangels, came to help me, and I left him there with the spirit prince of the kingdom of Persia.

Daniel 10:12–13

Daniel was unaware of what was going on in the spirit world during this time. Unbeknownst to him, the angel who brought this message from God to Daniel had been in a battle with another spiritual being, identified as the prince of the king of Persia. This was not a human being but a spirit. The entire time Daniel was fasting and praying, they were warring. The angel let Daniel know that God had heard his prayer from the first moment he prayed. However, it took twenty-one days to get to the breakthrough—his answer in the form of an angelic messenger—because of the spiritual warfare going on behind the scenes.

Friend, God hears you every time you pray. He hears you from the first moment you utter a word. Sometimes you will go through warfare on the way to getting that prayer answered. It often seems that when things can't get any worse, the answer comes. The old adage "It's always darkest just before dawn" is true. Don't let what you see with your eyes and hear with your ears dissuade you from pressing in. God hears. Your breakthrough could be just around the corner.

Spiritual Disciplines Are Crucial

Sometimes it's hard to respond in a godly manner when you're praying for justice to prevail. As you wait for the breakthrough, you will be tempted to respond in an un-Christlike fashion. There will be moments when it will take everything within you to refrain from sending a sarcastic text or rattling off a snarky social media post. It is important to saturate yourself in spiritual disciplines so that you are in the right frame of mind to respond righteously. Spiritual disciplines anchor you at all times, but especially when life is tumultuous and show no signs of calming down. When I have waited for wrongs to be righted, spiritual disciplines have kept me from making regrettable choices.

What are spiritual disciplines? Spiritual disciplines are practices in Scripture that help believers to grow in their spiritual journey. One of the best guides on spiritual disciplines is the classic *Celebration of Discipline* by Richard Foster. In his excellent overview of the disciplines, he lists inward disciplines, which include meditation, prayer, fasting, and study; outward disciplines, which include simplicity, solitude, submission, and service; and corporate disciplines, which include confession, worship, guidance, and celebration.[4]

I want to make particular mention about meditation as this is a confusing term for some. Even the word *meditation* can cause some Christians to recoil with concern about delving into a practice that is not godly, believing it is something reminiscent of Eastern religions and new age practices. For a long time, Christians have been robbed of an asset in their walk with God because of misunderstanding of what it means to meditate.

Foster explains the difference: "Eastern meditation is an attempt to empty the mind. Christian meditation is an attempt to fill the mind."[5]

Christian meditation involves filling the mind with the Word of God, and whatsoever things are true, honest, just, pure, lovely, and of good report (Philippians 4:8).

First Timothy 4:7 gives us a clear answer as to why spiritual disciplines are so important: "Discipline yourself for the purpose of godliness" (NASB). If the Holy Spirit dwells in you, godliness *is* your purpose, because He makes it so.[6] Discipline will bring us to that purpose of godliness.

There is no better way to stay on course spiritually—particularly through a crisis—than through the practice of spiritual disciplines.

Stay Under the Spout!

There have been times during worship and prayer at church when God was doing such a deep work in my heart that I thought to myself, *If I could just remain in this same atmosphere twenty-four seven, I could handle anything.* But of course, we can't stay in church services twenty-four seven, nor were we meant to. One day I had an epiphany about this.

I was boiling some pasta on the stove, went to drain it, and accidentally burned one of my fingers with scalding hot water. As long as I stood at the sink with cold water running over my finger, I didn't hurt. But as soon as I stopped, my finger throbbed terribly. I stood at the sink for a long time, but of course couldn't keep standing there forever. At some point, I stopped and bore the pain, and went back to what I was doing. The thought hit me: *What if I could remain under the spout of worship music and never leave it, particularly in my times of intense trials? How would this impact my ability to stand strong?*

Music has incredible power. Worship music, in particular, creates an atmosphere shift. In 2 Kings 3:15, Elisha said, "Bring me a musician," because he knew it was mood-shifting and he was setting the stage for a miracle. "Then it happened, when the musician played, that the hand of the LORD came upon him."

Although it's God who does the work, we need to set the stage. Worship music doesn't just set the stage for an uncommon answer to prayer, but it keeps us walking the right path. It keeps my head on straight when I'm dealing with unrighteous behavior and desire to respond in an ungodly fashion.

I made a playlist that was about eight hours long, containing mostly soaking types of worship, and started a practice of keeping it on at all times on my phone, day and night. It plays whether I am at work, grocery shopping, at the dentist, or anywhere else I go. During times of trial, it literally becomes the twenty-four seven backdrop of my life. It has been my saving grace many times in the midst of waiting for an answer to prayer and feeling like I can't stand one more minute of whatever it is I'm going through.

The feeling still comes occasionally. One day I said, "I can't handle one more minute of this!" And I sensed the Holy Spirit say to me, *You can do anything for one more minute, one more hour, one more day, one more year, or however long I tell you as long as you're in My presence.* The presence of God makes the difference in everything. We can run through a troop and leap over a wall if we need to (Psalm 18:29). In and of myself, I feel like nothing at times, but in God's presence, I feel unstoppable. You can be unstoppable, too—get under the spout!

— UNCOMMON TRUTHS for Uncommon Righteousness —

1. Waiting for wrongs to be exposed, or justice to be served, can feel excruciating, but remember that God is always working behind the scenes in ways that you are unaware of.

2. Instead of begging God to be on your side, get on His side.

3. The way to get on God's side is to live righteously. Being righteous means being right with God and doing right according to His Word—doing things His way.

4. Pay close attention to spiritual disciplines in your life, as they will give you a firm foundation and help you live righteously, especially in tough times such as when you are waiting for an answer from God for justice to be served.

5. Worship is an atmosphere shifter. You can do anything for one more minute, hour, day, year in the presence of God.

———— QUESTIONS for Reflection and Discussion ————

1. Was there ever a time when you were waiting for an answer to prayer for justice to be served? What was that period of time like for you?

2. Have you ever asked God to be on your side? What do you think it would be like to try getting on God's side instead?

3. What is your experience or habits concerning spiritual disciplines?

4. Have you ever kept worship music playing continually in order to create or shift an atmosphere in your life? What was the experience like?

5. Is social media a challenge for you (a temptation in any way) with situations where you are waiting for God to bring justice?

──────────── **ACTION STEP** ────────────

Take an inventory of the spiritual disciplines in your life. If reading God's Word has not been a regular practice for you, the best place to start is the Gospel of John. And how is your prayer life? If you have a hard time focusing, try writing your prayers in a notebook for just a few minutes every day.

10

UNCOMMON TEAMWORK

Homes, churches, or commercial buildings can take years to build. Some small construction projects can drag on for years. Yet one of the most iconic buildings in the world—a building that has been named one of the Seven Wonders of the Modern World by the American Society of Civil Engineers—was finished in a mere one year and forty-five days.

The address, 20 W. 34th Street, New York City, was the location of a quaint farm owned by John and Mary Murray in the late 1700s. It was the place where George Washington's troops retreated after a battle during the Revolutionary War. The Murrays sold the land to William Aldorf Astor, who built an upscale hotel on the site that lasted a little more than thirty years before the land was sold and the hotel demolished. The land was soon sold again to a group called Empire State, Inc., that had a goal to construct a building taller than any other in existence. At the time, it was widely believed to be impossible to build a structure taller than one hundred stories. The Empire State group set out to prove the world wrong by building a tower that would stand above every other.[1]

Two structures provided stiff competition—the Woolworth Building, which was 792 feet, and the Chrysler Building, at 1,046 feet. The Empire State group set a goal of building to 1,440 feet. The group pitched their structure to investors in early October 1929 as "a monument to the future."[2] But an incredible threat would emerge just a few weeks later. On that day, now known as Black Thursday, the stock market crashed, many banks and companies would fail, and the United States entered what would become known as the Great Depression.

The Empire State group remained undaunted. Despite the chaos that surrounded them, they broke ground on March 17, 1930. The majority of construction workers—3,439 of them, to be exact, at the peak of construction[3]—were eager European immigrants who worked together to accomplish this feat. The steelworkers and riveters soon became known as the "air-treaders" and "sky boys." *The New York Times* declared that they "put on the best open-air show in town."[4] These men defied gravity, balancing on narrow beams and hanging from lines, thousands of feet above the New York City streets. They would complete, on average, four and a half stories of the building each week. They faced intense physical labor, day after day, six days a week. Five workers lost their lives.

The building's completion in one year and forty-five days is still considered one of the most renowned architectural marvels of the world. When the Empire State Building officially opened on May 1, 1931, President Herbert Hoover turned on the lights by pressing a button in his office in the White House. History had been made! None of it would have been possible without the 3,439 workers who tirelessly served in unity of purpose to make the dream a reality. Teamwork was the key ingredient to this landmark building that today hosts over two and half million visitors a year and is the number one photographed building in the world.[5]

Nehemiah and the Wall

The air-treaders and sky boys weren't the first ones to get a world-renowned project done in record time. The rebuilding of the walls of Jerusalem, as told in the book of Nehemiah, was also a history-making feat.

Nehemiah was the cupbearer to the king of Persia, King Artaxerxes. The role of the cupbearer involved tasting the king's food and drink before it was served, to ensure that he was never poisoned. To be a cupbearer involved a high degree of trust, as the king's very life was in his hands. The role also entailed selecting the menu for the king and any guests at the table, and making sure it was to their liking. Being in proximity to the king on such an everyday basis, by default, made the cupbearer a person of influence. In his unofficial role, and life in general, Nehemiah was a servant, an influencer, and a leader. Keep in mind that leadership doesn't always come with an official title. It means personally, sometimes quietly, standing for what is right, regardless of those around you. It includes stepping out in the direction where God is leading, with the influence that He has given you.

Nehemiah discovered that the city walls of Jerusalem were still in ruins. Decades prior, the city had been destroyed, and even though the returned exiles had been there for years, no work had been accomplished—the walls were still just rubble, the gates in ashes. This was a serious problem. Today some people live in gated communities, but it isn't common or a necessity. In fact, fewer than one-fifth of Americans desire a gated community.[6] But in Nehemiah's day, city gates were essential. Having walls around the city was not about decor or aesthetics, but safety. A city without walls was vulnerable to every type of crime imaginable. People lived in a constant state of unrest and fear in a city without walls, and for good reason.

When Nehemiah found out about the ruins, he was so devastated that he immediately sat down and wept, mourned, fasted, and prayed—for days. Before entering the king's presence to seek permission to rebuild the walls, he prayed to God for favor.

> O Lord, please hear my prayer! Listen to the prayers of those of us who delight in honoring you. Please grant me success today by making the king favorable to me. Put it into his heart to be kind to me.
>
> Nehemiah 1:11

The king not only granted Nehemiah's request but asked how he could help. Nehemiah left what was considered an honored and prestigious role as cupbearer to the king, with the king's blessing and assistance, to lead the rebuilding of the wall.

And after arriving in Jerusalem and inspecting the wall, he included the Jewish leadership in the task of rallying to rebuild. Everyone worked together, breaking the rebuilding down into sections. Although the section teams were necessary, Nehemiah knew that the key—even more important than the power of teamwork—was to rely on God's power to accomplish the task. He said, "The God of heaven will help us succeed. We, his servants, will start rebuilding this wall" (Nehemiah 2:20).

Nehemiah and the teams worked under extreme pressure, and their lives were repeatedly threatened. But they were undaunted. Despite opposition, through prayer, the power of God, and teamwork, they were able to rebuild the walls of Jerusalem in a mere fifty-two days!

This story is just one example of how God works through both the natural and the supernatural. At one point, Nehemiah rallied the team to fight.

> As I looked over the situation, I called together the nobles and the rest of the people and said to them, "Don't be afraid of the enemy! Remember the Lord, who is great and glorious, and fight for your brothers, your sons, your daughters, your wives, and your homes!"
>
> Nehemiah 4:14

Then a bit further in the same chapter he says: "When you hear the blast of the trumpet, rush to wherever it is sounding. Then our God will fight for us!" (verse 20). Nehemiah understood the importance of the team doing what they could in the natural, and God taking care of the rest.

Just as some things will only happen with a combination of prayer and fasting, some extraordinary answers to prayer are only going to come through the power of teamwork. Jesus emphasized the importance of togetherness in Matthew 18.

> I also tell you this: If two of you agree here on earth concerning anything you ask, my Father in heaven will do it for you. For where two or three gather together as my followers, I am there among them.
>
> Matthew 18:19–20

God Has Often Worked Through Teams

Scripture is filled with examples of teamwork.

Moses and Aaron; David and Jonathan; Ruth and Naomi; Paul and Barnabas; Priscilla and Aquila; Paul and Timothy; Mary Magdalene, Joanna, and other women, to name a few. It was Jesus's custom to send the disciples out two by two: "And he called the twelve and began to send them out two by two, and gave them authority over the unclean spirits" (Mark 6:7 ESV).

Where the spiritual gifts are listed in 1 Corinthians 12, the body of Christ is compared to a human body, with each part having a significant and necessary role to play. It is clear that the kingdom of God was never meant to be about a one-star player, but a team of people working together.

Praying with others is not only powerful and effective, as James 5:16 tells us, but is also the greatest bonding experience. Charles Finney once noted, "Nothing tends more to cement the hearts of Christians than praying together. Never do they love one another so well as when they witness the outpouring of each other's hearts in prayer."[7]

Prayer Partnerships

There are a variety of ways to partner in prayer that are highly beneficial.

The advantage of praying with your spouse

If you are married, partnering with your spouse in prayer can be a catalyst for many breakthroughs in your marriage, family, and beyond. Throughout the years, people have asked for my husband's advice about the main qualities to look for in a spouse. He has answered, "I was looking for a woman who prays." He explained that he knew there would be times ahead when marriage would be rough and there would be disagreements. He said, "I knew if we were at an impasse, and I couldn't get through to my wife's heart on something, God could, especially if she was a woman who prayed." This has proven true for both of us.

If you are married, nothing is more important, or effective, than praying with your husband or wife. Author Megan Hill explains:

> As important as sexual intimacy is [between a husband and wife], the Lord allows one thing to occasionally eclipse it: "except . . . that you may devote yourselves to prayer." Praying together is so vital for married couples that if time and energy are in short supply, all other obligations should move down the to-do list.[8]

If you and your spouse are desperate for an answer to prayer as a couple, there is no greater strategy than partnering in prayer.

One of the things that has been helpful for Larry and me is to do daily devotions together on a Bible app. We take turns selecting a plan and then do that plan together over the coming days or week. At the end of each plan on the app we use, there is a section titled "Talk It Over." In this section we not only share our observations using the messaging feature of the app but also agree in prayer about things. We still pray together in person, but this is a powerful tool that keeps us connected every day, from anywhere in the world. When I travel for ministry, or am gone for days or even a week or two on missions, we stay intricately connected through daily devotions and prayer on this app. At times we find that writing our thoughts and prayers is even more sacred and intimate than if we had spoken them. And I appreciate being able to go back and reread what we have texted each other as we have come into agreement in prayer.

The advantage of praying with a friend

It's helpful to talk with your friends about your problems— God created us for community and bearing one another's burdens. I immediately feel lighter after I've shared my burden with a friend. But many times when I share a problem with a friend, I realize that while they can listen, and they can help me feel a bit lighter in spirit, they can't actually solve my problems in a practical way. There's another level available in friendship when that friend knows how to pray. The greatest friends are praying friends!

Friends who pray have been a part of my uncommon answers, time and again. Together, we can do what is guaranteed to make a difference—take that problem to the Lord and believe for it to be resolved. Being able to ask a friend for prayer in person, or online, is an absolute lifeline.

Ecclesiastes 4:9–12 explains:

> Two people are better off than one, for they can help each other succeed. If one person falls, the other can reach out and help. But someone who falls alone is in real trouble. Likewise, two people lying close together can keep each other warm. But how can one be warm alone? A person standing alone can be attacked and defeated, but two can stand back-to-back and conquer. Three are even better, for a triple-braided cord is not easily broken.

Scripture is making the point that sometimes the world can be cold and cruel, and the love and care of a friend is what brings warmth to life. We are better and stronger together, in prayer, and in every way.

The advantage of praying with a church family

The value of having a church family to pray with in times of need cannot be underestimated. "Call the prayer chain!" is something many believers remember hearing growing up, although in today's day and age, prayer needs are passed along via texting or online groups. Regardless of how the requests are shared, having a church family to call on is of immense value as members can readily mobilize to pray for urgent needs within the church community and beyond. Your church family joining you in prayer may hold the key to your uncommon answer.

To call on your church family, you need to have one! If you aren't already part of a solid church community, that is something to take care of immediately. Hebrews 10:24–25 explains the importance:

> Let us think of ways to motivate one another to acts of love and good works. And let us not neglect our meeting together, as some people do, but encourage one another, especially now that the day of his return is drawing near.

If you are able-bodied, go to church in person. And don't just attend—be an integral member of that church body. What you bring, as a unique individual, is an important contribution.

I recently saw a meme that illustrated an important point: "The next time your church has a dinner, watch it online and see how much you get fed." There is a significant difference between what you will receive online and what you receive in person. When you attend church, it is not exclusively about what you will receive, but also what you give to others. A word of encouragement, a hug, or joining with someone in prayer is an opportunity for a life-changing encounter for both you and the other person. Many people today, even when able-bodied, choose to be part of church online rather than in person. Some say, "The church is not a building." Consider that the church isn't a phone or a computer either. An electronic device isn't going to baptize you, anoint you with oil, serve you Communion, counsel you, marry you, bury you, or any of the other significant things that happen as a result of the ministry of the church. Being part of a healthy church family includes the benefits of corporate worship, a sense of belonging and community, support and encouragement, accountability, spiritual growth, and opportunities to be a part of service and outreach alongside your church family. You need a church, and a church needs you. Having a church family agree with you in prayer is only one of the many benefits of having a church to call home.

The advantage of a personal intercessor

There is great advantage in having a personal intercessor, particularly if you are a leader. Before I share what a personal intercessor is, it would be helpful first to tell you what it is not. A personal intercessor is not a therapist, counselor, pastor, or best friend. Although this person may have that role in a different area of their life, this is not part of their role as your personal intercessor. Simply defined, an intercessor goes before the Lord in prayer on behalf of another. A personal intercessor can be as valuable, if not more so, than your doctor or a professional counselor. While he or she does not take the place of these important individuals, they have a vital role, often alongside them. For example, I may say to my personal intercessor, "I have scheduled an appointment with my primary care doctor this week to discuss some concerning symptoms I am having. Will you please pray that she is able to get to the root of this issue and discover what is happening and what needs to be done?" My personal intercessor prays for healing of these symptoms, but she is also praying that God would lead and guide my medical doctor.

A personal intercessor must be a person of deep integrity, fully trustworthy, and extremely mature in their walk with the Lord. Prayer is their forte, and they take great delight in spending vast amounts of time in prayer on behalf of another. A personal intercessor does not take on this role for a leader in order to be close to him or her. Dr. Alice

Smith, who was the personal intercessor for the late C. Peter Wagner, wrote,

> Immature intercessors will often be so flattered by your invitation that they will jump at a chance to have "inside access" to you. In most cases they will become weary after a season, drop out from a sense of guilt and to keep from having to admit failure; this can result in lost church members as well.[9]

It is vitally important that personal intercessors be seasoned men and women of God. A personal intercessor who receives information from a leader takes it in and keeps it locked down as if it's in a vault. This individual has a track record of hearing clearly from God and can say hard things when necessary.

My personal intercessor is Cindy Georg. I can reach out at any time with prayer needs regarding my personal life, family, ministry or anything that encompasses my life. She is highly confidential and serves with integrity and the right motivation.

Cindy has been granted permission to speak into my life, to share not only the exciting things that will make me feel good—the things she sees down the road in the Spirit about what God wants to do—but also the pitfalls or hard things that I need to be aware of. For example, as I am sharing prayer needs with her and as she is praying for me, she might caution me against bitterness, reminding me that the enemy would love to entrap me and I must be careful not to take offense. One day when I was downtrodden about some issues, I shared them and asked her to pray. Cindy responded, "I sense the

Lord saying this is not the time right now to lament; it's a time to stand strong against the enemy's snares. This is not a time to cry, or mourn; it's a time to stand up and fight in the Spirit!"

I am so grateful for Cindy and her willingness to pray for me and to tell me the truth of what she sees in the Spirit. That is the reason this role is not for a spiritual novice.

One more thought: It is best to not choose someone for this role who comes to you and says, "I want to be your personal intercessor!" This is particularly true for a pastor, a pastor's spouse, or anyone who has a visible role in ministry. Many times, the individual does not have the right motivation. They are often either looking to be your best friend or to gain access to information that no one else knows. A good candidate for this role comes with no fanfare. They typically approach you humbly and discreetly, without pressure, saying things like, "I've been lifting you up in prayer. Let me know if there's anything specific you would like me to cover." In time, you will discover they can be trusted as you release more information to them, bit by bit. They will not get upset if you don't give them information. They consistently pray for you no matter what you share or don't share. They don't ask for private time with you to go for coffee or lunch, or to have private calls. They don't brag to others about how close they are to you.

Cindy is a great contributor to many of the uncommon answers to prayer that I have received. If you do not have a personal intercessor, rather than approach someone, pray for one. God is faithful to send just the right person.

The advantage of a prayer group

Being part of a prayer group is a superlative strategy for receiving answers to prayer. There is strength in numbers.

When a group joins in prayer, in alignment with God's will, anything is possible.

The story of the Tower of Babel in Genesis 11 was during a time when all the world's people spoke one language. They planned to build a tower to reach the sky, declaring in verse four:

> Come, let's build a great city for ourselves with a tower that reaches into the sky. This will make us famous and keep us from being scattered all over the world.

> The Lord saw what was about to happen.

> "Look!" he said. "The people are united, and they all speak the same language. After this, nothing they set out to do will be impossible for them! Come, let's go down and confuse the people with different languages. Then they won't be able to understand each other."

> Genesis 11:6–7

There is strength in numbers, whether for good or for bad. God knew that even when the people joined together for an ungodly purpose, they would get some traction in what they were trying to do.

As Christians, it must be our desire to be on the Lord's side, to align with His will, and pray that His purposes manifest in people and situations. There is great power when people unite and pray that God's will be done. There is a collective force that is much more potent than when people pray individually.

A prayer group serves as encouragement, support, and a faith-builder as members of the group spur one another on in prayer. For those who are not yet as strong in their faith, or even for seasoned Christians, a group encourages greater discipline in prayer habits. Joining together in prayer brings greater consistency to the prayer life of an individual than he or she would have alone. This is not unlike having a workout friend to help with accountability and consistency. As the prayer group experiences answers to prayer, they are encouraged all the more about the power of prayer. This is often impetus for new levels of individual and corporate growth within a prayer group and a church.

Joining forces with two or three or more is often the catalyst for uncommon answers that may not happen any other way.

When Two People Believed for a Thirty-Day Miracle

Martha Tennison and her husband, Don, served as lead pastors at several churches before becoming full-time evangelists. From 1973 to 1976 they pastored what was then known as Old Republican Assembly of God in Union City, Tennessee. Rose Warren was one of the faithful members of their church.

One day Rose shared with Martha that she was feeling extremely concerned about her husband, Ilar, who was not yet a believer. She had been hearing so much about how the rapture of the church could take place at any time, and she knew Ilar was not ready. As Rose was sharing her desire that her husband come to the Lord, Martha strongly sensed the Holy Spirit speak. She said, "Rose, would you be willing to agree with me for thirty days in prayer for Ilar's salvation? I am sensing the Lord saying that if we will agree together for thirty days, the Lord will save him." (Martha was careful to add that she sensed this was not to be misinterpreted as a doctrine—true for everyone—but as a specific word from God that she received for them.) Rose agreed to pray for thirty days, and that's exactly what they did.

On the thirtieth day, Rose called Martha and said, "I don't think anything's going to happen. He left the house grouchier than he's ever been."

Martha said, "Rose, the day isn't over until midnight! You keep praying and I'll keep praying."

When they hung up, Martha sensed an attack from the enemy in the form of: *What if something doesn't happen? What is she going to think of you?* Just as quickly, she also sensed the Lord's response: *I didn't call you to defend My word, Martha. I just told you to stand on it.*

At 11:55 p.m., the Tennisons' phone rang. "Who do you think that is?" Don said.

"It's Rose Warren!" responded Martha. When Martha answered, Rose, voice breaking with tears, said, "Sister Tennison, Ilar wants to get saved. Can you come to the house and pray with us?" The Tennisons quickly drove to the Warrens' home. When they arrived, Martha recalls with tears that she felt the presence of the Lord so strongly.

When they walked in, Ilar began to pour out his heart. "Pastor, I need help. I'm so miserable." Rose and the Tennisons joined together in leading Ilar in a prayer of salvation. A midnight-hour miracle.

Today, Ilar and Rose Warren are ninety and eighty-five years old, still living in Union City, Tennessee, and serving God together with all their hearts.

What might happen if you partnered in prayer with someone for your miracle?

—— **UNCOMMON TRUTHS for Uncommon Teamwork** ——

1. The kingdom of God was never meant to be about a one-star player, but a team of people working together.
2. The greatest friends are praying friends!
3. You need a church, and a church needs you.
4. If you are able-bodied, go to church in person. And don't just attend—be an integral member of that church body. What you bring, as a unique individual, is an important contribution.
5. A personal intercessor can be as valuable, if not more so, than your doctor or professional counselor. Not to take the place of them, but in addition to them.

———— **QUESTIONS for Reflection and Discussion** ————

1. Have you ever partnered with someone in prayer for a miracle? What was that process like for you?
2. Do you have a personal intercessor or someone whom you turn to with prayer requests regularly? If not, what are your thoughts on this? Is this something you would like to explore?
3. Have you been reluctant to share prayer requests in the past? If so, for what reason?
4. What do you believe might be possible by joining together with a friend in prayer?
5. Do you find yourself in a situation much like Rose Warren's? Is there a loved one for whom you need a miracle?

--- **ACTION STEP** ---

Find some way to prioritize corporate prayer in your life. If your church has a prayer service or group, support it with your attendance and participation. If your church has a prayer chain, join it. If your church has none of these things, maybe you could approach your pastor about starting one. Or consider starting one among friends who are part of neighboring churches.

11

UNCOMMON WARFARE

One of my favorite movies is *Schindler's List*, about German businessman Oskar Schindler who rescued 1,100 Jews from a Nazi concentration camp. It might seem odd that this is one of my favorites, given the horrific history that portrays some of the worst deeds of humanity. But Schindler's heroic efforts in saving so many people are inspiring. Another lesser-known hero who saved lives during that dark moment in history is Irena Sendler.

Irena Sendler was a Polish social worker with the Warsaw social services department during the Holocaust. She smuggled Jewish children to safety by finding non-Jewish homes for them where they would be hidden and protected from the Nazis. Sendler came up with an ingenious idea to save the children. She disguised herself as an infection-control nurse, and once she was welcomed inside a Jewish home, she would ask parents or grandparents to temporarily give up their children so she could take them to safety. After being transported to their new location, each child was given a new Polish name and personal identification papers. If Sendler could not find a non-Jewish home to shelter them, they would temporarily go to convents or orphanages. She was precise and strict about documentation, so that after the war children could be reunited with their parents. The documentation was hidden in milk jars that were buried in the backyard of one of her team members.

In 1943, Sendler was caught, arrested, and tortured by the Gestapo. No matter how horrific the treatment she received, she would not give up the names of her team members, nor reveal the identities of the children. She was rescued, and continued her work under a different identity. By the time the war was over, it was estimated that Irena Sendler had rescued 2,500 children.[1]

Irena Sendler accomplished extraordinary things, but she paid a high price to follow her passion for rescuing children. Similarly, whenever God is taking you in a new season or you are endeavoring to accomplish something great for Him, you can expect a level of unprecedented attack. When you first begin to encounter this as a believer, it can be quite a shock. It is essential to understand spiritual warfare and be prepared for it.

What Am I Doing Wrong?

No matter how long you have been a Christian, it can be easy to question why certain things are happening. It is common to wonder, *What have I done wrong to bring this on?* While it's always good to check ourselves and make sure we are obeying God in all things, it's also important to know that some attacks happen precisely because you're doing something right.

Perhaps no one in Scripture went through more spiritual warfare than Job. The Bible describes Job as a godly man of integrity who was blameless and stayed away from evil (Job 1:1). It's important to note that the Bible doesn't say he was sinless, but blameless. There is a difference. He wasn't a perfect man, but he was a really godly man. He had a wife, seven sons and three daughters, and was the wealthiest man in the area. As the story unfolds in the book of Job, we see that he was not only blameless but generous, with charitable deeds for the poor, disabled, and the orphaned. There was not an area in his life that was displeasing to God. Job was all that—a bag of chips and the Coke.

The Bible says one day Satan came before the Lord, who asked him where he had come from. He responded that he had been searching the earth, surveying what was happening. Then the Lord said to him,

> "Have you noticed my servant, Job? He is the finest man in all the earth. He is blameless—a man of complete integrity. He fears God and stays away from evil."
> Satan replied to the LORD, "Yes, but Job has good reason to fear God. You have always put a wall of protection around him and his home and his property. You have made him prosper in everything he does. Look how rich he is! But reach out and take away everything he has, and he will surely curse you to your face!"
> "All right, you may test him," the LORD said to Satan." "Do whatever you want with everything he possesses, but don't harm him physically."
>
> Job 1:8–12

And test him he did. Mercilessly.

In short order, all his oxen and donkeys were stolen, and the farmhands killed. Fire burned up his sheep as well as the shepherds. All of the camels were stolen and the servants killed. The horrific grand finale was a powerful wind that swept in and hit his house on all sides, collapsing it and killing all of his children.

Even after losing all of his possessions and his children, Job held tight to God. He stood up, tore his robe in grief, shaved his head, and fell to the ground in worship (verse 20). Then he said,

> I came naked from my mother's womb, and I will be naked when I leave. The LORD gave me what I had, and the LORD has taken it away. Praise the name of the LORD!
>
> Job 1:21

Job's very first reaction was not to lash out at God. Did he mourn? Yes. Mourning and lamenting is a godly practice. There is an entire book of the Bible about nothing but lament (Lamentations). Lament isn't terribly popular in the church today; there are few sermon series on it. This is unfortunate. So many times we try to skip over the crucifixion on the way to the resurrection. It's important to lament. Job lamented, but he didn't stay fixated on lamenting. Following it, he fell to the ground and worshipped. There is a time to weep and wail, and then a time to worship, get up, fight, and contend.

Following Job's lament and worship, Satan again visited the Lord, and again the Lord pointed out Job's integrity. Satan replied, "Skin for skin! A man will give up everything he has to save his life" (Job 2:4).

Any time we are physically impacted, our resolve to do anything can be weakened. It is typical for people in pain to lash out. God told Satan that he could test Job physically, but must spare his life. In response, Satan struck Job with painful boils from head to toe.

Job didn't have the ideal support system. Although his wife had been through the same devastations (and we should have compassion on her for that), she didn't share his level of faith. She told him he should curse God and die. His friends weren't much better. Although they deserve kudos for coming and sitting with him in silence for seven days and mourning with him, they ended up doing more harm than good. Once they started talking, it was to tell Job that he must have brought this upon himself. That he had caused all of this by sinning. They didn't believe all of it could happen "just because"—that Satan could have been allowed to send it without cause. Not only did Job's friends give completely unworkable advice, but their words made things worse. In response, Job told them they were miserable comforters. Yet they persisted, and Job's faith did not waver.

In my opinion, one of the most outstanding moments in the Bible is when God rebuked Job's friends. He commanded them to sacrifice a burnt offering to atone for their actions. And then, in one of the best plot twists ever, when Job prayed for his friends, God restored all of his fortune. Here are the glorious details:

> The LORD restored the fortunes of Job when he prayed for his friends, and the LORD increased all that Job had twofold. . . . The LORD blessed Job in the second half of his life even more

than in the beginning. For now he had 14,000 sheep, 6,000 camels, 1,000 teams of oxen, and 1,000 female donkeys. He also gave Job seven more sons and three more daughters. He named his first daughter Jemimah, the second Keziah, and the third Keren-happuch. In all the land no women were as lovely as the daughters of Job. And their father put them into his will along with their brothers. Job lived 140 years after that, living to see four generations of his children and grandchildren. Then he died, an old man who had lived a long, full life.

Job 42:10,12–17

Job is a perfect example that at times it seems as though we've got to go through hell to get to heaven. Are we willing to pay a price?

God never intended for Job's experience to be just the story of one man's devastating life experiences. You can't really niche down his problem to physical suffering, financial ruin, or other factors. This book is primarily a theological manifesto on suffering, and what to do when things don't make sense. Job had to wrestle with the fact that he—as a godly, blameless man— was going through hell on earth. We can learn vicariously through him.

Sometimes we pay the price for victory in the level of spiritual warfare we are willing to endure. When I first began to draft this book, I sensed God saying to me, "Are you ready for the price you will have to pay to write this book?" I knew exactly what that meant, for I had experienced paying the price not only in prayer but in spiritual warfare in many other God-assignments.

The Day from Hell

There was a day that my husband and I refer to as the "day from hell." I woke up and immediately knew there was something wrong. My husband was not next to me in bed. I have over an hour commute to my office, and I wake up and leave the house in the mornings much earlier than he does. I went to the family room and found him sitting with our dog, Max. I asked him what was wrong, and he said he had not been able to sleep. He was awake most of the night, concerned about our church's finances. After a hurricane earlier in the year, we had to cancel several weeks of services, and there were also repairs to be made on the building. The church was behind financially, and he was worried. He said, "I've called a board meeting so that I can inform the leaders, pray about it together, and get direction." I told him I was sorry things had come to this point but that I would pray along with him and believe God to intervene.

I arrived at my office, and midmorning my husband called, extremely stressed. His primary care doctor called with the news that some lab reports had come back that were alarming. He asked my husband to come to his office immediately to go over the reports and get prescriptions. After that visit, with my husband still trying to process everything, his dermatologist called to say that a biopsy had come back indicating he had cancer that would require several surgeries. I could hear the heaviness in Larry's voice. "Deanna," he said, "I just don't know how much more I can take today. I'm heading over to drop Max off at the vet for his shots and then I'll go to the office. Please, please pray for me. I am feeling so overwhelmed." I prayed for him right there over the phone and reassured him as best I could. Then my assistant, Judi, and I headed out for lunch.

Our meals had just been delivered to the table when my cell phone rang. It was Larry. He was crying. I have only heard my husband cry a few times in decades of marriage. Now he was sobbing. I asked what in the world was going on, and through broken sobs he told me that during Max's routine visit, the vet noticed something curious about one of his legs. After examining it, she told Larry she was certain Max had bone cancer. She expected him to live six months or less. Larry was so overcome with emotion he said he didn't know how he was going to drive home. Judi and I immediately boxed up our lunches and I went home.

I couldn't imagine the day getting any worse, but the most terrible part had not yet happened. I knew that Larry was in no shape to preach for the Wednesday night service, so I encouraged him to ask our oldest son to preach. I would go to church and open the service and handle everything aside from the message. He could stay home and try to recover a bit from what had been a terrible day. He agreed to do so. That went well. But that night, something happened that was like a bomb going off in our family.

It is not my story to tell, so I am not sharing the details out of respect. What I can share is that life would not be the same, or even okay, for an exceedingly long time. Larry and I were both so shocked that we held each other and cried— sometimes in the middle of the night, for months to come. We fiercely clung to each other as the bottom dropped out of our world. I met with my boss and asked if I should resign. Before I could even get all the words out of my mouth, he said, "No! Absolutely not. This is not your fault, and it is not the time for you to step down." He was so gracious and encouraging.

When our day from hell was over, the fire continued, unfortunately. We would walk through many challenging moments that stretched us to the limit. Max died very quickly from cancer. But we also had so much to give God praise for amid the pain that was still present in our family situation. Larry recovered from two surgeries and worked hard to reverse his diagnosis. He did so, receiving a clean bill of health. The church finances turned around. We steadily plodded forward with prayer, fasting, and doing all that we knew to do in the natural and the spiritual.

An Aha Moment

There are times that we forget how crafty the enemy is, and how he aims to steal, kill, and destroy (John 10:10). You can be a Christian for a long time—even a strong intercessor— and this can still slip your mind.

During the year all this was taking place, I was steadily moving toward one of the biggest breakthroughs in the ministry I lead for women in the state of Florida. Over my years of serving as director, our ministry had grown to the point where our fall conference was outgrowing the different hotel ballrooms where we were meeting. At the previous year's conference, we were fewer than one hundred women away from exceeding the limit per fire code regulations. Something had to be done. For me, that something needed to be a decision that *wasn't* capping the attendance. Not because we wanted to boast about numbers, but because women's lives were being transformed. Every year at the conference, hundreds of women were saved, filled with the Spirit, and experienced miracle healings of every kind. We also had ministry for teen girls. I couldn't envision closing the attendance and not being able to reach every woman or girl who desired to attend.

We looked into the Daytona Ocean Center Arena for the next year's conference. They would only offer us a two-year contract. They wouldn't let us try it for a year to see if we could handle it financially. What if we didn't have enough in attendance to cover the cost of this additional space? We sensed God's leading, the contract was signed, and we proceeded.

Karen Wheaton and her daughter, Lindsey Doss, were two of our keynote speakers. As we customarily do, our team fasted and prayed for thirty days before the conference for all of the spiritual transformations we desired to see happen.

On the opening night, Karen and Lindsey arrived at the arena shortly after worship began. They entered the back of the room and paused before going to their reserved seats at the front. Surveying the scene, Karen leaned over to Lindsey and said, "This has been fasted over—I can tell!" They could both sense the heavy anointing in the room. From the get-go, even before any speaker took the stage or a word was preached, women streamed forward to the altars, pressing in to receive from God. It was evident that the women would not have to be primed to enter in and receive.

What happened in the arena that weekend was otherworldly. Hundreds of women received Christ, and signs, wonders, and miracles were in abundance. Women and girls repented of sin and were set free. At one point, Karen felt the Holy Spirit leading her to bring a huge clay pot to the edge of the stage. She encouraged women who had a relationship that needed to be surrendered to God—one that was not pleasing to Him—to write a goodbye note and leave it there, symbolically surrendering the relationship. One of the speakers had shared about her affair, and how God had restored her marriage. Hundreds of women came streaming to the front to drop their goodbye notes into the pot. Later, before destroying the notes we glanced through the pile. They were full of letters that said things like, "Goodbye, Sean, our affair is *over*. I've surrendered to Jesus." and "Goodbye, Tyler, we are through. I am getting right with Jesus today." That one altar service was the beginning of many marriages being restored.

It was a good thing we moved to the arena, because hundreds of women were added to our number that year. Countless women would not have received their miracle had we stayed in the hotel ballrooms.

During the conference I was able to spend a few moments alone at lunch with Karen and Lindsey. As we talked, I shared what our family had been going through in our day from hell. Karen looked at me wide-eyed, leaned across the table, and said, "Deanna, you do know why you're going through all this, right?"

"No, please tell me," I said.

"It's because of what you're carrying." (By this, she meant it was a personal attack on my life because of what I was carrying on behalf of all those who would be touched by God at this event and our ministry as a whole.) She continued, "There's a price to be paid for what is happening here. Thousands of lives are changing for the glory of God, and the enemy isn't just going to sit idly by and let this happen.

What better way for him to attack this ministry than to attack your family? Than to tempt you to quit?" Karen and Lindsey reminded me that the stakes were high, and the enemy doesn't play fair.

Through years of fasting and prayer and implementing all of the spiritual strategies I have shared in this book, our family situation has improved. We have had breakthroughs and forward movement as we have sought God. I will continue implementing all these things until I take my last breath.

Partnering with the Holy Spirit to receive uncommon answers is not always quick, nor easy. A good friend of mine often reminds people that Jesus is coming back for a church "without spot or wrinkle"—and how do you get wrinkles out? Heat and pressure. There are times the heat and pressure feel unbearable as we pray. But we can be encouraged by Galatians 6:9: "So let's not get tired of doing what is good. At just the right time we will reap a harvest of blessing if we don't give up."

——— UNCOMMON TRUTHS for Uncommon Warfare ———

1. You don't have to do wrong to come under attack. Sometimes it is because you are doing right.
2. The enemy is our constant accuser, waiting for our faith to fail under fire.
3. At times we will be misunderstood and ill-advised by our family and friends, even by those who are closest to us.
4. There is a price to be paid for spiritual breakthrough.

5. Continuing to stand in the gap (pray for others) even though they may be coming against you moves the heart and hand of God.

QUESTIONS for Reflection and Discussion

1. Have you personally experienced spiritual warfare before or after major spiritual breakthrough?
2. How can we be a better support to our friends who are going through warfare?
3. How have you struggled with what God causes versus what He allows?
4. What are some things you have found helpful in staying strong and standing firm through times of spiritual attack?
5. Are you experiencing spiritual attack right now?

ACTION STEP

Ephesians 6:10–18 instructs us to put on the full armor of God, and stay ready for battle. Read this passage today, then write or print it out. Place it somewhere in your home or work environment where you can be reminded of the need to stay spiritually ready for battle at all times.

12

FIGHTING FOR YOUR UNCOMMON ANSWER

Fighting for your uncommon answer to prayer is not a once-and-done event. Living in the extraordinarily more that Jesus has for you is a lifestyle. As mind-blowing as this is, Jesus has called you to do things He did while He was here in the flesh—and greater things! Listen to John 14:11–14 in *The Message*:

> Believe me: I am in my Father and my Father is in me. If you can't believe that, believe what you see—these works. The person who trusts me will not only do what I'm doing but even greater things, because I, on my way to the Father, am giving you the same work to do that I've been doing. You can count on it. From now on, whatever you request along the lines of who I am and what I am doing, I'll do it. That's how the Father will be seen for who he is in the Son. I mean it. Whatever you request in this way, I'll do.

You are destined for greater things. The type of things Jesus is interested in—the things that have His heart. In fact, He says you can count on it. Anything you ask along the lines of who He is and what He's doing—He'll do it! If that doesn't make you get up off the couch and run around the room, I don't know what will! But you've got to do just that—get up and go. As Frederick Douglass said, you've got to put legs on your prayers. Putting the legs on your prayers takes listening, waiting, hard choices, surrender, obedience, sacrifice, tenacity, righteousness, teamwork, and warfare. A believer who uses these God-strategies on a regular basis is unstoppable.

The Holy Spirit is with you. Partner with Him to receive extraordinarily more. Your uncommon answer is on the way!

ACKNOWLEDGMENTS

Mary DeMuth at Mary DeMuth Literary, my dream agent, for taking a chance on me, believing in me, pouring into me, and encouraging me. I am ever grateful for your mentorship.

David Sluka, former acquisitions editor at Chosen/Baker Publishing, for giving me this opportunity, hearing my heart for this book, and responding in such a way that was yet another uncommon answer in my life. You will always be special to me because you took a chance on me.

Jill Olson, editor extraordinaire, for making the editing process so enjoyable. Thank you for making the book so much better.

Deirdre Close and the marketing team at Chosen/Baker Publishing, for all the things you did to set up *Uncommon Answers* for success, and for being so kind and giving throughout the entire journey.

Kim Bangs, editorial director at Chosen, for all of your support in the process.

All my family and friends—your names could take up several pages if I listed you all. Thank you for loving me and believing in me.

And most of all, thank You, Holy Spirit—the best friend I have ever had, and ever will have.

NOTES

Introduction

1. Isabelle Benarous, *The Bio-Breakthrough: Decode Your Illness and Heal Your Life* (Bioprogramming Press, 2020), 9.

Chapter 1 Uncommon Answers Don't Have to Be Rare

1. Albert Barnes, "Commentary on Acts 10," *Barnes' Notes on the Whole Bible* (1870), https://www.studylight.org/commentaries/eng/bnb/acts-10.html.

2. Mark Batterson, *The Circle Maker: Praying Circles Around Your Biggest Dreams and Greatest Fears*, Enhanced Edition (Zondervan, 2011), 82.

3. Frederick Douglass, "Self-Made Men," *New York Daily Herald*, November 16, 1876, https://www.loc.gov/resource/sn83030313/1876-11-16/ed-1/?sp=5&st=image.

Chapter 2 Uncommon Listening

1. Rebecca Ripley, "We're Learning—Are you Listening?," Chief Learning Officer, May 7, 2024, https://www.chieflearningofficer.com/2014/05/07/were-learning-are-you-listening.

2. Emi Jozuka and Pete Muntean, "Japan Coast Guard Plane Not Cleared for Takeoff Before Deadly Runway Crash, Air Traffic Control Transcript Suggests," CNN, January 4, 2024, https://www.cnn.com/2024/01/03/asia/japan-plane-crash-transcript-intl/index.html.

3. Olivia Munson, "Titanic Sinking: Here's What to Know About Why the Famous Ship Went Down," *USA Today*, April 15, 2024, https://www.usatoday.com/story/news/2023/09/14/why-did-the-titanic-sink/70383448007.

4. Rebecca Morelle, Alison Francis, and Gareth Evans, "Titan Sub CEO Dismissed Safety Warnings As 'Baseless Cries,' Emails Show," *BBC News*, June 23, 2023, https://www.bbc.com/news/world-us-canada -65998914.

5. Julie True is known for ministering in Spirit-led soaking worship music that creates an atmosphere of peace and comfort through anointed spontaneous soaking worship soundscapes. You can find out more about her at JulieTrue.com.

Chapter 3 Uncommon Waiting

1. Jason Farmen, "Is Waiting a Lost Art?," *Knowledge at Wharton*, January 27, 2024, https://knowledge.wharton.upenn.edu/podcast /knowledge-at-wharton-podcast/slowing-down-why-good-things-come -to-those-who-wait.

Chapter 4 Uncommon Choices

1. *Encyclopedia of World Biography*, "Mother Teresa Biography," accessed January 27, 2024, https://www.notablebiographies.com/Mo-Ni /Mother-Teresa.html; Vatican, "Mother Teresa of Calcutta (1910–1997)," October 18, 2003, https://www.vatican.va/news_services/liturgy/saints /ns_lit_doc_20031019_madre-teresa_en.html.

2. Serekara Gideon Christian and Baribefe Daniel Koate, "The Haematological Perspective of the Biblical Woman with Issue of Blood," *Nigerian Biomedical Science Journal* 14 (2017), https://www.research gate.net/publication/339299241_The_Haematological_Perspective _of_The_Biblical_Woman_with_issue_of_Blood_by_Serekara_Gideon _Christian_Baribefe_Daniel_Koate.

3. *Thayer's Greek Lexicon*, "G3958, paschō," Blue Letter Bible, accessed January 27, 2024, https://www.blueletterbible.org/lexicon/g3958 /kjv/tr/0-1.

4. Teen Challenge is a Christian drug rehabilitation program that is widely known and utilized in our ministerial circles. They have a tremendous track record of success.

5. For more information on fasting, I highly recommend Jentezen Franklin's book *Fasting: Opening the Door to a More Intimate, More Powerful Relationship with God* (Charisma House, 2017).

Chapter 5 Uncommon Surrender

1. Dennis Cruywagen, *The Spiritual Mandela: Faith and Religion in the Life of Nelson Mandela* (Imagine, 2018).

2. Saugato Biswas, Trupti Surana, Abhishek De, and Falhuni Nag, "A Curious Case of Sweating Blood," *Indian Journal of Dermatol* 58, no. 6 (2013), 478–480, https://www.ncbi.nlm.nih.gov/pmc/articles /PMC3827523.

Chapter 6 Uncommon Obedience

1. *Encyclopedia Britannica*, "Battle of Thermopylae," by Kate Lohnes and Donald Sommerville, last updated September 17, 2024, https://www.britannica.com/event/Battle-of-Thermopylae-Greek-his tory-480-BC.

2. Edward W. Klink III, "An Exegetical Reading of the Wedding at Cana (John 2:1–11)—An Excerpt from John," *Zondervan Academic* (blog), January 6, 2017, https://zondervanacademic.com/blog/an-exege tical-reading-of-the-wedding-at-cana-john-21-11-an-excerpt-from-john.

3. Oswald Chambers, *The Pilgrim's Song Book* in *The Complete Works of Oswald Chambers* (Discovery House, 2000), 537.

Chapter 7 Uncommon Sacrifice

1. Loyola Press, "Saint Monica," accessed March 9, 2024, https:// www.loyolapress.com/catholic-resources/saints/saints-stories-for-all -ages/saint-monica.

2. Names and identifying details in this story have been changed.

Chapter 8 Uncommon Tenacity

1. Daphne Myers, "Wilma Rudolph: Champion and Role Model," David C. Cook, accessed April 4, 2024, https://ministryspark.com/wp -content/uploads/21-WilmaRudolph.pdf.

2. Arlisha R. Norwood, *Wilma Rudolph*, National Women's History Museum, 2017, https://www.womenshistory.org/education-resources /biographies/wilma-rudolph.

3. Janet Lee, "Is Tenacity Born or Made?," Nike, September 12, 2022, https://www.nike.com/a/is-tenacity-born-or-made.

4. The Vineyard Movement started in the mid-1970s and resulted in the Association of Vineyard Churches.

5. Now called Evangel University.

Chapter 9 Uncommon Righteousness

1. *PBS News Hour*, "The Medgar Evers Assassination," April 18, 2002, https://www.pbs.org/newshour/nation/media-jan-june02-evers_04-18.

2. Jerry Mitchell, "On This Day in 1994," On This Day, *Mississippi Today*, February 5, 2023, https://mississippitoday.org/2023/02/05/on-this -day-byron-de-la-beckwith.

3. All names and identifying information in this story have been changed.

4. Richard Foster, *Celebration of Discipline: The Path to Spiritual Growth*, anniv. ed. (HarperOne, 2018), 6.

5. Foster, *Celebration of Discipline*, 20.

6. Donald S. Whitney, *Spiritual Disciplines for the Christian Life* (NavPress, 1991), 3.

Chapter 10 Uncommon Teamwork

1. "Constructing History," The Empire State Building, accessed August 13, 2024, https://www.esbnyc.com/about/history.

2. Emily Bice, "The Complete History of the Empire State Building," *CitySignal*, December 27, 2022, https://www.citysignal.com/empire-state -building-history-facts.

3. Thomas Kelly, "Performing Miracles, with Wrench and Rivet," *New York Times*, April 23, 2006, https://www.nytimes.com/2006/04/23/nyreg ion/nyregionspecial5/performing-miracles-with-wrench-and-rivet.html.

4. Harry He, "The Empire State Building: Crafting the 8th World Wonder," Walks, last updated December 12, 2023, https://www.takewalks .com/blog/how-was-the-empire-state-building-built.

5. "Facts and Figures," The Empire State Building, accessed April 19, 2024, https://www.esbnyc.com/about/facts-figures.

6. Elana Ashanti Jefferson, "Americans Are Leaving Gated Communities," *Denver Post*, March 12, 2007, https://www.denverpost.com/2007 /03/12/americans-are-leaving-gated-communities.

7. Charles Grandison Finney, *Lectures on Revivals of Religion* (Fleming H. Revell, 1835), 114.

8. Megan Hill, *Praying Together: The Priority and Privilege of Prayer in our Homes, Communities, and Churches* (Crossway, 2016), 117–118.

9. Alice Smith, "What Leaders Need from Their Intercessors," Healthy Leaders, November 28, 2018, https://healthyleaders.com/leaders-need -intercessors.

Chapter 11 Uncommon Warfare

1. Jack Mayer, "Irena Sendler and the Girls from Kansas," *Humanities* 41, no. 3 (2020), https://www.neh.gov/article/irena-sendler-and-girls -kansas.